D1570783

Essential Papers on
Transference Analysis

Essential Papers on Transference Analysis

edited by
Gregory P. Bauer, Ph.D.

JASON ARONSON INC.
Northvale, New Jersey
London

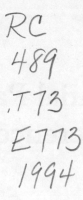

RC
489
.T73
E773
1994

This book was set in 11 point Palacio by Lind Graphics of Upper Saddle River, New Jersey, and printed and bound by Haddon Craftsmen of Scranton, Pennsylvania.

Library of Congress Cataloging-in-Publication Data

Essential papers on transference analysis / edited by Gregory P.
  Bauer.
    p. cm.
   This edited collection of papers . . . represents a companion
edition to . . . The analysis of the transference in the here and now —
Pref.
   Includes bibliographical references and index.
   ISBN 0-87668-529-7 (softcover)
   1. Transference (Psychology) 2. Psychotherapy. 3. Resistance
(Psychoanalysis) I. Bauer, Gregory P. II. Bauer, Gregory P.
Analysis of the transference in the here and now.
   [DNLM: 1. Transference (Psychology) — collected works.
2. Psychoanalytic Interpretation — collected works. WM 62 E77 1994]
RC489.T73E773 1994
616.89'14 — dc20
DNLM/DLC
for Library of Congress   93-8962

Manufactured in the United States of America. Jason Aronson Inc. offers books and cassettes. For information and catalog write to Jason Aronson Inc., 230 Livingston Street, Northvale, New Jersey 07647.

To my parents,

Frank and Patricia

Contents

Preface

This edited collection of papers on transference and psycho-therapy represents a companion edition to my text *The Analysis of the Transference in the Here and Now*. These papers are meant to review transference, highlight the importance of its here-and-now analysis, and identify patient and therapist resistance to this process. With each I have provided an overview and synopsis to elucidate points most pertinent to analysis of transference in the here and now. Transference can be a powerful therapeutic tool; it behooves us to continue to examine the phenomenon and refine its application.

SECTION I

THE ANALYSIS OF TRANSFERENCE IN THE HERE AND NOW

In many ways . . . the discovery of transference gave definitive meaning and function to psychoanalytic therapy, and however modified in recent years, remains at the heart of analytic work.

Robert Langs, 1981, p. 3*

Transference was originally viewed as an intrapsychic experience of the patient unrelated to the actual person of the therapist. Neutral, opaque, and relatively unobtrusive, the therapist was a figure upon whom the patient projected unresolved libidinal and aggressive conflicts of an oedipal nature. The patient's experience in therapy was thought to be detached from the actual presence of the therapist.

As the phenomenon evolved, transference began to take on a more interpersonal and interactional cast. The therapist was increasingly viewed as a participant–observer, affecting, as well as

---

*Robert Langs, *Classics in Psychoanalytic Technique* (New York: Jason Aronson, 1981).

being affected by, the patient. Not solely a projection of unconscious impulses onto a blank screen, transference was something created in the present, emanating from the patient–therapist interchange. The product of this interchange was often found to resemble the patient's characteristic means of reacting and interacting with others. The patient was seen as behaving in a way to elicit responses from the therapist consistent with the patient's view of self and others, and reinforcing of his neurosis. As transference became increasingly understood as an interpersonal and interactional as well as intrapsychic phenomenon, its analysis evolved from a rather singular focus on the genesis of inner psychological conflict to include a more active and collaborative examination of the development and character of the patient–therapist interaction. This approach has been termed *the analysis of transference in the here and now* and is characterized by use of the current relationship to identify, examine, and modify self-defeating patterns of interpersonal relatedness as they are expressed within the therapeutic dyad.

Papers selected for this section illustrate the steady expansion, clarification, and revision of the concept of transference analysis. To provide the reader with a classical perspective of transference, the section begins with Freud's (1912) delineation of the concept. The papers that follow reflect the growing appreciation for an interpersonal and interactional approach to transference. A contemporary overview of transference is offered by Westen (1988). A paper by Wolf (1966) follows in which he explores the development of impaired interpersonal relations and how they may be modified by means of the patient–therapist interaction. The therapist as a participant–observer and a more flexible use of neutrality are topics of Wachtel (1986). In the next paper, Hoffman (1983) emphasizes the astuteness of patient perception and the need to approach transference analysis in a collaborative manner. To Hoffman, transference entails (1) selective attention; (2) predisposition to interpret behavior in a characteristic manner; and (3) the tendency to provoke behavior consistent with one's expectations. The section concludes with

Gill's (1979) suggestions on how transference analysis may be improved. Resistance to transference, and transference as resistance are differentiated and discussed. The resistance of both patient and therapist to a here-and-now focus is highlighted.

1

The Dynamics of Transference*

Sigmund Freud

EDITOR'S SYNOPSIS

With this paper Freud lays groundwork for understanding the nature of transference and its role in analytic treatment. Transference is seen to occur as a result of unsatisfied libidinal need, which compels the patient to seek attachment to the analyst. In this attachment the analyst is experienced in a manner similar to how an earlier significant other has been experienced. The phenomenon of transference is seen to represent a most powerful resistance to analysis, whereas in other therapies it is regarded as the vehicle of cure. The patient is viewed as resisting conscious recognition of repressed, conflict-laden impulses by acting them out in his relationship with the therapist. This

---

*This paper was published in the *Standard Edition*, 1912; 12: 97–108.

resistance to awareness, understanding, and change is thought to be omnipresent and to accompany the treatment step by step. Every act of the patient is seen to reflect a compromise between forces striving for recovery and those wishing to maintain the status quo.

Freud felt that the resistive nature of transference could be best understood by identifying the various components of transference. He distinguished a positive transference from a negative (hostile) one. Positive transference was further differentiated into friendly, affectionate feelings, which are mature, goal-limited, and reality-oriented, and those feelings that are of a more obvious erotic nature. Freud thought that negative and erotic transference obstructed the analytic process. Negative transference was thought to distance the patient from the therapist; erotic transference precluded a focus on real-life problems. While recommending analysis of these two components of transference, Freud thought that the transfer of warm, affectionate feelings facilitated treatment in that they could be used to induce the patient to accomplish the work of therapy.

Freud notes the difficulties involved in interpretation of transference. Unconscious impulses do not want to be remembered in the way the analyst wishes but endeavor to reproduce themselves. While the patient regards feelings for the analyst as contemporaneous and real, the analyst encourages him to examine them in light of his life history and the therapy situation. This struggle between analyst and patient, between understanding and acting out, finds expression in the phenomenon of transference. While presenting the analyst with his greatest difficulties, transference performs the service of making hidden conflicts immediate, apparent, and available for therapeutic intervention.

This paper represents a landmark contribution to the psychoanalytic literature. Containing the seeds of many ideas/advances that were carefully nurtured by future theorists, it is to be read and reread.

The almost inexhaustible topic of transference has recently been dealt with by Wilhelm Stekel in this journal[1] on descriptive lines. I should like in the following pages to add a few remarks to explain how it is that transference is necessarily brought about during a psycho-analytic treatment, and how it comes to play its familiar part in it.

It must be understood that each individual, through the combined operation of his innate disposition and the influences brought to bear on him during his early years, has acquired a specific method of his own in his conduct of his erotic life—that is, in the preconditions to falling in love which he lays down, in the instincts he satisfies and the aims he sets himself in the course of it.[2] This produces what might be described as a stereotype plate

---

[1] The *Zentralblatt für Psychoanalyse*, in which the present paper first appeared.

[2] I take this opportunity of defending myself against the mistaken charge of having denied the importance of innate (constitutional) factors because I have stressed that of infantile impressions. A charge such as this arises from the restricted nature of what men look for in the field of causation: in contrast to what ordinarily holds good in the real world, people prefer to be satisfied with a single causative factor. Psychoanalysis has talked a lot about the accidental factors in aetiology and little about the constitutional ones; but that is only because it was able to contribute something fresh to the former, while, to begin with, it knew no more than was commonly known about the latter. We refuse to posit any contrast in principle between the two sets of aetiological factors; on the contrary, we assume that the two sets regularly act jointly in bringing about the observed result. Δαίμων καὶ Τύχη [Endowment and Chance] determine a man's fate—rarely or never one of these powers alone. The amount of aetiological effectiveness to be attributed to each of them can only be arrived at in every individual case separately. These cases may be arranged in a series according to the varying proportion in which the two factors are present, and this series will no doubt have its extreme cases. We shall estimate the share taken by constitution or experience differently in individual cases according to the stage reached by our knowledge; and we shall retain the right to modify our judgement along with changes in our understanding. Incidentally, one might

(or several such), which is constantly repeated—constantly re-printed afresh—in the course of the person's life, so far as external circumstances and the nature of the love-objects accessible to him permit, and which is certainly not entirely insusceptible to change in the face of recent experiences. Now, our observations have shown that only a portion of these impulses which determine the course of erotic life have passed through the full process of psy-chical development. That portion is directed towards reality, is at the disposal of the conscious personality, and forms a part of it. Another portion of the libidinal impulses has been held up in the course of development; it has been kept away from the conscious personality and from reality, and has either been prevented from further expansion except in phantasy or has remained wholly in the unconscious so that it is unknown to the personality's con-sciousness. If someone's need for love is not entirely satisfied by reality, he is bound to approach every new person whom he meets with libidinal anticipatory ideas; and it is highly probable that both portions of his libido, the portion that is capable of becoming conscious as well as the unconscious one, have a share in forming that attitude.

Thus it is a perfectly normal and intelligible thing that the libidinal cathexis of someone who is partly unsatisfied, a cathexis which is held ready in anticipation, should be directed as well to the figure of the doctor. It follows from our earlier hypothesis that this cathexis will have recourse to prototypes, will attach itself to one of the stereotype plates which are present in the subject; or, to put the position in another way, the cathexis will introduce the doctor into one of the psychical "series" which the patient has already formed. If the "father-imago," to use the apt term introduced by Jung, is the decisive factor in bringing this about, the outcome will tally with the real relations of the subject to his doctor. But the transference is not tied to this particular proto-type: it may also come about on the lines of the mother-imago or brother-imago. The peculiarities of the transference to the doctor,

_____

venture to regard constitution itself as a precipitate from the accidental effects produced on the endlessly long chain of our ancestors.

thanks to which it exceeds, both in amount and nature, anything that could be justified on sensible or rational grounds, are made intelligible if we bear in mind that this transference has precisely been set up not only by the *conscious* anticipatory ideas but also by those that have been held back or are unconscious.

There would be nothing more to discuss or worry about in this behaviour of transference, if it were not that two points remain unexplained about it which are of particular interest to psycho-analysis. Firstly, we do not understand why transference is so much more intense with neurotic subjects in analysis than it is with other such people who are not being analysed; and secondly, it remains a puzzle why in analysis transference emerges as *the most powerful resistance* to the treatment, whereas outside analysis it must be regarded as the vehicle of cure and the condition of success. For our experience has shown us—and the fact can be confirmed as often as we please—that if a patient's free associations fail[3] the stoppage can invariably be removed by an assurance that he is being dominated at the moment by an association which is concerned with the doctor himself or with something connected with him. As soon as this explanation is given, the stoppage is removed, or the situation is changed from one in which the associations fail into one in which they are being kept back. At first sight it appears to be an immense disadvantage in psychoanalysis as a method that what is elsewhere the strong-est factor towards success is changed in it into the most powerful medium of resistance. If, however, we examine the situation more closely, we can at least clear away the first of our two problems. It is not a fact that transference emerges with greater intensity and lack of restraint during psycho-analysis than out-side it. In institutions in which nerve patients are treated non-analytically, we can observe transference occurring with the greatest intensity and in the most unworthy forms, extending to nothing less than mental bondage, and moreover showing the plainest erotic colouring. Gabriele Reuter, with her sharp powers

---

[3]I mean when they really cease, and not when, for instance, the patient keeps them back owing to ordinary feelings of unpleasure.

of observation, described this at a time when there was no such thing as psycho-analysis, in a remarkable book which betrays in every respect the clearest insight into the nature and genesis of neuroses.[4] These characteristics of transference are therefore to be attributed not to psycho-analysis but to neurosis itself.

Our second problem—the problem of why transference appears in psycho-analysis as resistance—has been left for the moment untouched; and we must now approach it more closely. Let us picture the psychological situation during the treatment. An invariable and indispensable precondition of *every* onset of a psychoneurosis is the process to which Jung has given the appropriate name of *introversion*[5] That is to say, the portion of libido which is capable of becoming conscious and is directed towards reality is diminished, and the portion which is directed *away* from reality and is unconscious, and which, though it may still feed the subject's phantasies, nevertheless belongs to the unconscious, is proportionately increased. The libido (whether wholly or in part) has entered on a regressive course and has revived the subject's infantile imagos.[6] The analytic treatment

---

[4]*Aus guter Familie*, Berlin, 1895.

[5]Even though some of Jung's remarks give the impression that he regards this introversion as something which is characteristic of dementia praecox and does not come into account in the same way in other neuroses. [This seems to be the first published occasion of Freud's use of *introversion*. The term was first introduced by Jung in 1910, but Freud is probably criticizing Jung's 1911 article. Some further comment on Jung's use of the term will be found in a footnote to a 1913 technical paper as well as in Freud's paper on narcissism (1914, *Standard Edition*, 14) and in a passage towards the end of Lecture XXIII of the *Introductory Lectures* (1916–17). Freud used the term extremely seldom in his later writings.]

[6]It would be convenient if we could say "it has recathected his infantile complexes." But this would be incorrect: the only justifiable way of putting it would be "the unconscious portions of those complexes." The topics dealt with in this paper are so extraordinarily involved that it is tempting to embark on a number of contiguous problems whose clarification would in point of fact be necessary before it would be

now proceeds to follow it; it seeks to track down the libido, to make it accessible to consciousness and, in the end, serviceable for reality. Where the investigations of analysis come upon the libido withdrawn into its hiding-place, a struggle is bound to break out; all the forces which have caused the libido to regress will rise up as "resistances" against the work of analysis, in order to conserve the new state of things. For if the libido's introversion or regression had not been justified by a particular relation between the subject and the external world—stated in the most general terms by the frustration of satisfaction[7]—and if it had not for the moment even become expedient, it could never have taken place at all. But the resistances from this source are not the only ones or indeed the most powerful. The libido at the disposal of the subject's personality had always been under the influence of the attraction of his unconscious complexes (or, more correctly, of the portions of those complexes belonging to the unconscious), and it entered on a regressive course because the attraction of reality had diminished. In order to liberate it, this attraction of the unconscious has to be overcome; that is, the repression of the unconscious instincts and of their productions, which has meanwhile been set up in the subject, must be removed. This is responsible for by far the largest part of the resistance, which so often causes the illness to persist even after the turning away from reality has lost its temporary justification. The analysis has to struggle against the resistances from both these sources. The resistance accompanies the treatment step by step. Every single association, every act of the person under treatment must reckon

---

possible to speak in unambiguous terms of the psychical processes that are to be described here. These problems include the drawing of a line of distinction between introversion and regression, the fitting of the theory of complexes into the libido theory, the relations of phantasying to the conscious and the unconscious as well as to reality—and others besides. I need not apologize for having resisted this temptation in the present paper.
    [7][See the full discussion of this in the paper on "Types of Onset of Neurosis" (1912)].

with the resistance and represents a compromise between the forces that are striving towards recovery and the opposing ones which I have described.

If now we follow a pathogenic complex from its representation in the conscious (whether this is an obvious one in the form of a symptom or something quite inconspicuous) to its root in the unconscious, we shall soon enter a region in which the resistance makes itself felt so clearly that the next association must take account of it and appear as a compromise between its demands and those of the work of investigation. It is at this point, on the evidence of our experience, that transference enters on the scene. When anything in the complexive material (in the subject-matter of the complex) is suitable for being transferred on to the figure of the doctor, that transference is carried out; it produces the next association, and announces itself by indications of a resistance— by a stoppage, for instance. We infer from this experience that the transference-idea has penetrated into consciousness in front of any other possible associations *because* it satisfies the resistance. An event of this sort is repeated on countless occasions in the course of an analysis. Over and over again, when we come near to a pathogenic complex, the portion of that complex which is capable of transference is first pushed forward into consciousness and defended with the greatest obstinacy.[8]

After it has been overcome, the overcoming of the other portions of the complex raises few further difficulties. The longer an analytic treatment lasts and the more clearly the patient realizes that distortions of the pathogenic material cannot by themselves offer any protection against its being uncovered, the

---

[8]This, however, should not lead us to conclude in general that the element selected for transference-resistance is of peculiar pathogenic importance. If in the course of a battle there is a particularly embittered struggle over the possession of some little church or some individual farm, there is no need to suppose that the church is a national shrine, perhaps, or that the house shelters the army's pay-chest. The value of the object may be a purely tactical one and may perhaps emerge only in this one battle.

more consistently does he make use of the one sort of distortion which obviously affords him the greatest advantages—distortion through transference. These circumstances tend towards a situation in which finally every conflict has to be fought out in the sphere of transference.

Thus transference in the analytic treatment invariably appears to us in the first instance as the strongest weapon of the resistance, and we may conclude that the intensity and persistence of the transference are an effect and an expression of the resistance. The *mechanism* of transference is, it is true, dealt with when we have traced it back to the state of readiness of the libido, which has remained in possession of infantile imagos; but the part transference plays in the treatment can only be explained if we enter into its relations with resistance.

How does it come about that transference is so admirably suited to be a means of resistance? It might be thought that the answer can be given without difficulty. For it is evident that it becomes particularly hard to admit to any proscribed wishful impulse if it has to be revealed in front of the very person to whom the impulse relates. Such a necessity gives rise to situations which in the real world seem scarcely possible. But it is precisely this that the patient is aiming at when he makes the object of his emotional impulses coincide with the doctor. Further consideration, however, shows that this apparent gain cannot provide the solution of the problem. Indeed, a relation of affectionate and devoted dependence can, on the contrary, help a person over all the difficulties of making an admission. In analogous real situations people will usually say: "I feel no shame in front of you: I can say anything to you." Thus the transference to the doctor might just as easily serve to *facilitate* admissions, and it is not clear why it should make things more difficult.

The answer to the question which has been repeated so often in these pages is not to be reached by further reflection but by what we discover when we examine individual transference-resistances occurring during treatment. We find in the end that we cannot understand the employment of transference as resistance so long as we think simply of "transference." We must make up our minds to distinguish a "positive" transference from a "negative" one, the transference of affectionate feelings from that of hostile ones, and to treat the two sorts of transference to the doctor separately. Positive transference is then further divisible into transference of friendly or affectionate feelings which are admissible to consciousness and transference of prolongations of those feelings into the unconscious. As regards the latter, analysis shows that they invariably go back to erotic sources. And we are thus led to the discovery that all the emotional relations of sympathy, friendship, trust, and the like, which can be turned to good account in our lives, are genetically linked with sexuality and have developed from purely sexual desires through a softening of their sexual aim, however pure and unsensual they may appear to our conscious self-perception. Originally we knew only sexual objects; and psycho-analysis shows us that people who in our real life are merely admired or respected may still be sexual objects for our unconscious.

Thus the solution of the puzzle is that transference to the doctor is suitable for resistance to the treatment only in so far as it is a negative transference or a positive transference of repressed erotic impulses. If we "remove" the transference by making it conscious, we are detaching only these two components of the emotional act from the person of the doctor; the other component, which is admissible to consciousness and unobjectionable, persists and is the vehicle of success in psycho-analysis exactly as it is in other methods of treatment. To this extent we readily admit that the results of psycho-analysis rest upon suggestion; by suggestion, however, we must understand, as Ferenczi does, the influencing of a person by means of the transference phenomena which are possible in his case. We take care of the patient's final independence by employing suggestion in order to get him to accomplish a piece of psychical work which has as its necessary result a permanent improvement in his psychical situation.

The further question may be raised of why it is that the resistance phenomena of transference only appear in psychoanalysis and not in indifferent forms of treatment (e.g., in institutions) as well. The reply is that they do show themselves in these other situations too, but they have to be recognized as such. The breaking out of a negative transference is actually quite a common event in institutions. As soon as a patient comes under the dominance of the negative transference he leaves the institution in an unchanged or relapsed condition. The erotic transference does not have such an inhibiting effect in institutions, since in them, just as in ordinary life, it is glossed over instead of being uncovered. But it is manifested quite clearly as a resistance to recovery, not, it is true, by driving the patient out of the institution—on the contrary, it holds him back in it—but by keeping him at a distance from life. For, from the point of view of recovery, it is a matter of complete indifference whether the patient overcomes this or that anxiety or inhibition in the institution; what matters is that he shall be free of it in his real life as well.

The negative transference deserves a detailed examination, which it cannot be given within the limits of the present paper. In the curable forms of psychoneurosis it is found side by side with the affectionate transference, often directed simultaneously towards the same person. Bleuler has coined the excellent term *ambivalence* to describe this phenomenon.[9] Up to a point, ambivalence of feeling of this sort seems to be normal; but a high degree of it is certainly a special peculiarity of neurotic people. In obsessional neurotics an early separation of the "pairs of opposites"[10] seems to be characteristic of their instinctual life and

---

[9]Bleuler, 1911. Cf. a lecture on ambivalence delivered by him in Berne in 1910, reported in the *Zentralblatt für Psychoanalyse*, 1. Stekel has proposed the term *bipolarity* for the same phenomenon. [This appears to have been Freud's first mention of the word *ambivalence*. He occasionally used it in a sense other than Bleuler's, to describe the simultaneous presence of active and passive impulses. See an Editor's footnote, *Standard Edition*, 14.]

[10][The pairs of opposite instincts were first described by Freud in his *Three Essays* (1905), *Standard Edition*, 7, and later on in "Instincts and their Vicissitudes" (1915), *Standard Edition*, 14. Their importance in obsessional neurosis was discussed in the "Rat Man" case history (1909), *Standard Edition*, 10.]

to be one of their constitutional preconditions. Ambivalence in the emotional trends of neurotics is the best explanation of their ability to enlist their transference in the service of resistance. Where the capacity for transference has become essentially limited to a negative one, as is the case with paranoics, there ceases to be any possibility of influence or cure.

In all these reflections, however, we have hitherto dealt only with one side of the phenomenon of transference; we must turn our attention to another aspect of the same subject. Anyone who forms a correct appreciation of the way in which a person in analysis, as soon as he comes under the dominance of any considerable transference-resistance, is flung out of his real relation to the doctor, how he feels at liberty then to disregard the fundamental rule of psycho-analysis[11] which lays it down that whatever comes into one's head must be reported without criticizing it, how he forgets the intentions with which he started the treatment, and how he regards with indifference logical arguments and conclusions which only a short time before had made a great impression on him—anyone who has observed all this will feel it necessary to look for an explanation of his impression in other factors besides those that have already been adduced. Nor are such factors far to seek: they arise once again from the psychological situation in which the treatment places the patient.

In the process of seeking out the libido which has escaped from the patient's conscious, we have penetrated into the realm of the unconscious. The reactions which we bring about reveal at the same time some of the characteristics which we have come to

---

[11][This seems to be the first use of what was henceforward to become the regular description of the essential technical rule. A very similar phrase ("the main rule of psycho-analysis") had, however, been used already in the third of Freud's Clark University Lectures (1910), *Standard Edition*, 11. The idea itself, of course, goes back a long way; it is expressed, for instance, in Chapter II of *The Interpretation of Dreams* (1900), *Standard Edition*, 4, in essentially the same terms as in the paper "On Beginning the Treatment" (1913), where, incidentally, the subject will be found discussed in a long footnote.]

know from the study of dreams. The unconscious impulses do not want to be remembered in the way the treatment desires them to be, but endeavour to reproduce themselves in accordance with the timelessness of the unconscious and its capacity for hallucination.[12] Just as happens in dreams, the patient regards the products of the awakening of his unconscious impulses as contemporaneous and real; he seeks to put his passions into action without taking any account of the real situation. The doctor tries to compel him to fit these emotional impulses into the nexus of the treatment and of his life-history, to submit them to intellectual consideration and to understand them in the light of their psychical value. This struggle between the doctor and the patient, between intellect and instinctual life, between understanding and seeking to act, is played out almost exclusively in the phenomena of transference. It is on that field that the victory must be won—the victory whose expression is the permanent cure of the neurosis. It cannot be disputed that controlling the phenomena of transference presents the psycho-analyst with the greatest difficulties. But it should not be forgotten that it is precisely they that do us the inestimable service of making the patient's hidden and forgotten erotic impulses immediate and manifest. For when all is said and done, it is impossible to destroy anyone *in absentia* or *in effigie*.

---

[12][This is elaborated in a later technical paper "Recollecting, Repeating and Working-Through" (1914).]

2

Transference and Information Processing[1]

Drew Westen

EDITOR'S SYNOPSIS

In this paper Westen reviews transference in a manner that integrates cognitive-behavioral and psychoanalytic perspectives. In doing so the concept is made palatable to many not typically identified as psychodynamic. Westen uses such terms as *person schema, scripts,* and *interpersonal expectancies* to put transference in an idiom readily assimilated by a wide audience, thus increasing its utility. This assimilation is further supported by the empirical evidence Westen provides for numerous analytic concepts (e.g., unconscious process). The article offers opportunity for further mastery to the psychodynamically inclined therapist as well. Westen notes that the term *transference* can become problematic in that it may be used to refer to many different phenomena including feelings about the therapist, behavior patterns toward

[1]This paper was published in *Clinical Psychology Review*, 1988; 8:161–179.

the therapist, and expectations of people in general. Through his discussion of the various phenomena that fall under the rubric of transference, Westen helps the therapist to become more precise about what experience is being focused on. This leads to greater clarity of thinking and improved communication—patient to therapist and therapist to therapist.

Westen examines how the interpersonal process between patient and therapist may be used to facilitate change. He views a focus on the patient–therapist interaction as a means of identifying the patient's typical interpersonal scripts, assumptions about the world, and inclinations toward others. These are traced to underlying cognitive and emotional schema. Helping the patient become more aware of these schema allows for examination and, if necessary, modification. The transference relationship is viewed as having the potential to activate affects associated with unresolved conflict that, while repressed, continue to affect present behavior. Identifying these affects and tracing them to their source helps bring conflict into consciousness and affords the patient an opportunity to examine childhood fears and expectancies with one's adult ego.

In regard to here-and-now work, Westen observes that use of the transference relationship to identify interpersonal expectancies, and to demonstrate that one's fears as to what may happen in relationships are not necessarily valid, is similar to in vivo exposure techniques in behavioral treatments. Activating real feelings and interaction patterns is viewed as having more impact than merely talking about them. Bridging the gap between the cognitive and analytic thinking on transference in a manner that does justice to both, Westen provides further clarification of concept without detracting from its richness.

The play's the thing wherein I'll catch the conscience of the king.
—*Hamlet*

For when all is said and done, it is impossible to destroy anyone *in absentia* or *in effigie*.
—Sigmund Freud

I was recently referred for projective testing of a woman who was hospitalized for depression and possible borderline personality disorder. The first session proceeded rather uneventfully; she had a jaded, cynical style about her and tended to give up on tasks when she had the slightest reason to believe that she might not complete them successfully. When I returned for the second session, it was clear that she would not give me any more information unless I backed away from the more rigid testing format and simply talked with her for a while. After doing so for a half an hour, we returned to the testing, at which point she proceeded to keep me for 2 hours in order to complete a test that normally takes about 30 minutes. At the end of the session, having manipulated me into staying (in various only dimly masked ways), she denounced me as a liar for having kept her beyond the hour-and-a-half that I had, the previous day, forecast for the second session.

The process I had just experienced with this patient was far more useful diagnostically than a Minnesota Multiphasic Personality Inventory (MMPI) profile, a Hamilton depression score, or a set of Thematic Apperception Test (TAT) responses. I came out of the session feeling as if I had victimized her, while in reality I had merely administered a standard battery of psychological tests. The theme of victimization permeated both the content and process of the testing, as she presented herself as a person who pushes people away with derision and cynicism in order to protect herself from the abuse she expects to receive. The extent to which she does this in all relationships obviously cannot be assessed in her interaction with a single tester in a single situation, but the fact that she turned a situation that most patients find somewhat anxiety-provoking—but basically benign—into a battle to protect herself from abuse clearly suggests something regarding the nature of her assumptions about the social world. The relatively brief relationship between this woman and myself thus proved to be a useful tool for the assessment of her object relations or "interpersonal schemata."

Repeated encounters such as this led Freud to focus, as early as 1895, on the relationship between therapist and patient, and to the notion of transference. Freud noticed that the attitude of the patient toward the therapist continually kept interfering with the business at hand of uncovering memories and associations. Eventually, he came to conclude that this peculiarity of the analytic situation is not in fact a hindrance but instead represents a fundamental part of the therapeutic process.

The aim of this paper is to reanalyze the concept of transference from an information-processing perspective and to show, from that perspective, how utilization of the interpersonal process between patient and therapist can be therapeutically useful. The purpose of applying information-processing theory and research to the concept of transference is twofold. First, it provides an empirical grounding to a basic psychoanalytic concept, and demonstrates, using experimental research that is likely to be more convincing to empirically oriented clinicians and researchers, that transference phenomena not only occur but are therapeutically useful. In so doing, it puts transference notions into a language compatible with the understanding of a vast number of therapists (and cognitive psychologists) who do not otherwise find the psychoanalytic notion of transference compelling, and thus allows a greater number of practitioners to make use of a crucial therapeutic tool. Secondly, it offers a way of explaining transference that many psychodynamic clinicians may find useful, which retains the psychoanalytic understanding of unconscious motivational processes and intrapsychic transformations without invoking a problematic tension-release, drive-discharge model of motivation that leaves many forms of adaptive behavior unexplained. In so doing, it tries to show how one can develop a more fine-grained understanding of transference by analyzing the specific information-processing mechanisms involved.

The article will begin by summarizing very briefly the psychoanalytic theory of transference. It will then apply recent research on information processing and social cognition to the concept of transference and delineate six components of the transference process. Finally, it will attempt to integrate cognitive and psychodynamic concepts to demonstrate the importance of transference in psychotherapy as a mechanism for the assessment and alteration of dysfunctional scripts, expectancies, and wishes; the uncovering of state-dependent memories and schema-triggered affects; and the reworking of maladaptive modes of affect-regulation. It will argue that to work therapeutically without utilizing transference phenomena is to discard a useful source of data and an important tool for therapeutic change.

TRANSFERENCE IN PSYCHOANALYTIC PSYCHOLOGY

While Freud first introduced the concept of transference in his *Studies on Hysteria* (1895) and discussed it again in the Dora case (1905), his first systematic treatment of the subject appeared in a 1912 essay in which he argues that people carry with them certain "stereotype plates" that determine their later erotic interests. He asserts that part of those templates is conscious and not immune to change, whereas another part, which forms the basis for transference, remains inaccessible to consciousness and impervious to development. In that essay he introduces the notion of transference as a resistance, arguing that patients use transference feelings to distract them from conflictual issues. He ascribes in that essay an enormous role to transference in psychotherapy, arguing that the resolution of transference is synonymous with the resolution of neurosis (p. 101).

In a later paper (1915) he grapples with the relationship between transference–love and normal love and argues that transference–love is never related to aspects of the present situation and instead is "entirely composed of repetitions and copies of earlier reactions . . ." (p. 167). In that essay he reiterates the therapeutic importance of working with transference, asserting that "the only really serious difficulties" the analyst must face "lie in the management of the transference" (p. 159).

In his *Introductory Lectures on Psychoanalysis*, Freud (1917) provides the first comprehensive definition of transference:

We mean a transference of feelings on to the person of the doctor since we do not believe that the situation in the treatment could justify the development of such feelings. We suspect, on the contrary, that the whole readiness for these feelings is derived from elsewhere, that they were already prepared in the patient and, upon the opportunity offered by the analytic treatment, are transferred on to the person of the doctor. [p. 442]

The patient's relationship to the therapist, he contends, stirs "new editions of the old conflicts," and the function of examining the transference is to help the patient reevaluate these conflicts as an adult and revise previous repressions (p. 454). He returns to the same theme 20 years later in his last important discussion of transference (1937), arguing that analysis of transference is central to the mechanism of therapeutic change, which entails the "replacement [owing to the strengthening of the ego] of the inadequate decision made in infancy by a correct solution" (p. 321). He is arguing, in essence, that what seems frightening to a child and sets in motion various more or less automatic defenses to reduce the fear may not be frightening to an adult. Thus, by examining the conflict and the defense consciously as an adult, the person may find that the fear which elicited the defense is unrealistic, and that he therefore need not distort himself to protect against it.

Currently, psychodynamic clinicians tend to use the term *transference* in one of two ways. They either use it narrowly to refer strictly to the transferring of thoughts, feelings, and fantasies about some childhood figure onto the therapist; or broadly, to refer to any aspect of the interpersonal process between patient and therapist. This latter is the sense in which the term *counter-transference* is often used to refer to any emotional reaction the patient evokes in the therapist. (For more recent thought on transference, see Gill 1982.)

INFORMATION PROCESSING AND THE COMPONENTS OF TRANSFERENCE

The psychoanalytic theory of transference leaves several important questions unresolved. The first pertains to the generality of a patient's reaction to the therapist. The notion of transference as it has been used often does not distinguish between relatively circumscribed responses cued by specific features of the therapist or therapeutic situation, as opposed to more global responses that may be triggered in many or most interpersonal interactions or are uniquely reactivated in the therapy situation. As Wachtel (1981) has pointed out, clinicians tend not to look at the particular stimuli that elicit transference phenomena at a given point in a given therapy.

A second issue relates to the distinction between transference and any other bond of affection. Freud (1915) argued that transference involves the reactivation of archaic imagoes and is thus, unlike real love, unrelated to the present reality. The problem with this is that, as Freud pointed out, every object finding is in some sense a refinding; to distinguish between reality elements and infantile elements is thus difficult in both theory and practice because any adult attachment is the end-product of a history of prior attachments.

Finally, the suggestion that therapeutic work is completed with the resolution of the transference is problematic, as Freud (1937) himself came to acknowledge. Freud's contention that all neurotic conflict becomes transferred onto the person of the analyst rests less upon clinical practice and observation than upon a theory of psychic energy that many in the psychoanalytic community now reject (e.g., Holt 1976). Freud argued that the libido attached to the neurotic symptoms detaches itself from the symptoms and reattaches itself to the analyst in the course of the treatment. Without this assumption, one has little reason to believe that all of the patient's conflicts come to revolve around the analyst so that resolving the transference would mean resolving the neurosis.

Many of these problems stem from the use of the term *transference* to refer to many different phenomena, including thoughts about the therapist, feelings about the therapist, expectations of the therapist, expectations of people in general, thoughts and feelings about the therapist that are *analogous* to early thoughts and feelings, thoughts and feelings about the therapist that are *homologous* or identical to early such thoughts and feelings, behavior patterns toward the therapist, resistance, erotic interest, and so forth. These difficulties can be ameliorated by applying ideas from cognitive psychology to the concept of transference[2] and separating out several distinct phenomena that are related to one another but not isomorphic.

Before doing so it is important to note the parameters within which information-processing concepts can be expected to be useful. The notion that people form representations of social and nonsocial objects and ideas is central to both cognitive psychology and psychoanalysis, as is the concept of associational networks that link various representations. To the extent that information-processing psychologists have developed methods for the rigorous study of these phenomena, their research can certainly be expected to enrich clinical understanding.[3] Similarly, recent research on social cognition and on cognitive-affective interactions undertaken from an information-processing perspective should be of enormous interest to psychoanalytically oriented clinical

---

[2]Since this article was written, Singer (1985) has published an excellent paper in which he relates concepts of schema, script, and expectancy to the psychoanalytic notion of transference.

[3]Landau and Goldfried (1981) have recently discussed the assessment of schemas in psychotherapy from a cognitive-behavioral standpoint.

psychologists. Studies of social-cognitive development (Shantz 1983), for example, are clearly of relevance to object relations theory (see Westen 1985).

The limitation of information-processing psychology for clinical and psychoanalytic theory and practice stems from the limits imposed by a computer metaphor: computers do not feel or wish. Cognitive psychology has yet to grapple with questions of motivation, though the recent turn to the study of cognitive-affective interactions holds the promise of future integrations of our knowledge of cognition and psychodynamics. This article represents an effort in that direction.

Transference as Person Schema/Object Representation

The concept of "schema" has a long history, dating back to Piaget (1926) and Bartlett (1932), and it is currently being put to widespread use by social cognition researchers (e.g., Taylor and Crocker 1980). Within academic psychology, Cantor and Mischel (1979) have argued that people tend to form prototypes for categorization of classes of people, and that the more the characteristics of a given person fit prototypical features, the more likely the stimulus person is to be treated as a member of that class. Within psychoanalysis, object relations theorists have similarly focused for decades on mental representations of social objects.

Piaget emphasized that forming an understanding in a given domain is an active process, and this is true in social cognition as in any other area of schema-building. A patient is always going to form a schema/object-representation of what the therapist is like, and this schema is likely to be distorted for both cognitive and motivational reasons, just as any social schema (or self-schema) is distorted. In terms of cognitive biases, Nisbett and Ross (1980) have catalogued a host of such sources of error in person perception, and it is the fate of creatures who must construct their understanding of reality that their constructions will always be imperfect. From the motivational side, patients have any number of reasons to distort their perceptions of their therapists, some of which will be detailed below. For example, they may idealize the therapist in order to identify with him or her, or they may vilify her in order to avoid hearing something painful she or he has to say. Though one may be tempted to restrict the use of the word transference to schemas distorted by motivational factors, as Wachtel (1981) argues, separating reality from distortion in defining transference is no easy task, since in any relationship neither party has a monopoly on objectivity, and ambiguity calling for inference is the rule, not the exception.

Various social schemas become transferentially relevant when they are evoked because of similarity to the therapist or some situational cue. To the extent that the manner or appearance of the therapist resembles another person or exemplar of a category, schemas relevant to that person or category are likely to be activated. Freud (1912) had just such a scenario in mind when discussing how a father image could be activated in the course of therapy. Over an extended period of time the therapist is likely to see the activation of many such schemas and to become aware of patterns in their elicitation. Once the schema is activated, the person is likely to ignore details of the therapist's behavior that do not fit the schema, as numerous studies have demonstrated the tenacity of schemas and the tendency to assimilate and selectively attend rather than to accommodate (see, e.g., Markus 1977, on the tendency to recall confirming evidence).

Not only may characteristics of the therapist evoke prior person schemas, but aspects of the therapeutic situation itself may do so. Cantor and colleagues (1982) have proposed that people construct situation prototypes, and to the extent that features of the therapy situation meet prototypical features, the person is likely to assimilate the current situation to old schemas. Patients frequently discuss feeling judged by therapists who maintain a nonjudgmental stance; telling one's inner thoughts and confessing wishes and deeds to someone in a position of authority and with whom one has an asymmetrical relationship evokes various parental and other authority prototypes. One patient, when discussing his feelings toward therapy or toward me, would frequently shift into talking about his relationships with his students. Putting aside for a moment whatever dynamic significance that may have had, at a strictly cognitive level he appears to have assimilated therapy to his "school schema." He informed me during one session that he felt very uncomfortable in therapy because he wanted me to correct his character like one would criticize a paper, by marking "good" by certain parts and red-penciling others that could use some improvement. If only I would do that, he thought, he could quickly revise those characterological sentence splices. He commented that he finds the lack of explicit expectations on my part unnerving, adding that his students know precisely what they must do to receive a good grade. In this case an elaborate schema has been evoked, and one has reason to suspect that earlier aspects of the schema in which he was a pupil rather than teacher were operative as well.

Transference as Attachment

A second aspect of transference is the patient's attachment to the therapist. One could account for this attachment in a number of ways. First, as Bowlby (1969, 1973) and others (e.g., Sroufe and Waters 1979) have argued, human beings appear to have an innately based tendency to form attachments, and that a person would do so in a relationship that fits a number of person and situation prototypes of early attachments is not surprising. Freud meant by his comment that every object finding is really an object re-finding that we learn to love in the context of our early relationships with our caretakers, and that the understanding we form of love is forever conditioned by these experiences. From a cognitive perspective, one can readily see how one schema builds upon the next developmentally, and how early images of relationships may be integrated into later schemas. This is by no means to deny that significant accommodation occurs along the way; rather, it is to suggest that prototypes of love objects and modes of attaching formed in infancy and childhood are likely to exert influence on subsequent object choices because old schemas never die: they fade away through disuse, are incorporated in various ways into subsequent schemas, or are repressed and periodically activated without conscious awareness.

As I have argued elsewhere (Westen 1985), one need not accept the more mechanistic aspects of Freud's drive theory to believe in the impact of early object relations on later social experience. One could argue, instead, that human infants have a genetically wired tendency toward social behavior and attachment, and that this differentiates into various social needs (including friendship, love, intimacy, sexual intimacy, etc.), rather than that all such needs are manifestations of the sexual instinct. Any of these needs may be evoked in psychotherapy, so that one would expect to see, for example, erotic transferences as well as simple attachments to the therapist. As will be argued shortly, these various needs are likely to call upon similar information-processing channels, so that in many cases they can be expected to arise in conjunction with one another.

Attachment to the therapist may arise through a second way. As Zajonc (1968) has shown, familiarity tends to lead to liking, and to the extent that the therapist becomes a familiar figure, he is likely to evoke positive feeling. A third way, symptom reduction, if attributed to therapy, will lead to attachment as the therapist becomes associated with relief, although the opposite side of this coin is that anxiety experienced in therapeutic work also becomes associated with the therapist (and frequently is responsible for premature terminations). Finally, telling intimate details of one's life to another person is likely to evoke schemas previously associated with attachment, such as parental schemas and "close friend" schemas.

Transference as Schema-Triggered Affect

Clinicians frequently speak of transference when a patient expresses positive or negative feelings toward the therapist. The patient may develop both continuous and momentary feelings toward the therapist just as he would toward anyone else. These feelings must obviously be understood in the context of the person's prior experience, as resulting from interactions between that experience and the current situation. Affects may be triggered directly by schemas activated through their perceived similarity to aspects of the therapist or therapy situation. Fiske (1982) has developed the notion of schema-triggered affect, by which she means that when features of a stimulus match characteristics of a cognitive prototype, the affect associated with the previous schema will be activated. In other words, classes of stimuli—and she studied social stimuli in particular—have affects attached, so that presentation of a member of that class will evoke the category-based affect. This is, of course, a phenomenon stereotype researchers (and victims of stereotypes) have known for decades. A member of a minority group may find that those around him begin with negative feelings toward him simply because they have attached an affect to a category, and he is an instance of that category.

Fiske performed a series of experiments that demonstrated that the greater the number of prototypic features that characterize the stimulus person, the more likely is schema-based affect to be triggered, and degree of affect varies by degree of association (i.e., number of shared attributes). According to Fiske, "When new information can be fit into old affectively laden knowledge, then the person has available an immediate affective response" (p. 57).

In psychotherapy an affect may be triggered in precisely this way. The patient may not always be aware of the category that is being triggered; she may simply experience the affect and have no awareness of the schema to which she has assimilated something in the therapy situation. Assumptions about unconscious processes of this sort, essential to clinical understanding, have recently received considerable experimental support. Shevrin and Dickman (1980) and Nisbett and Wilson (1977) have impressively demonstrated the extent of cognitive processing of which a person is not aware, and the likelihood is high that recognition of categorical processing may be an experience to which the individual is not introspectively privy and can only reconstruct post facto. If such is the case, an important aspect of therapeutic work may be to explore associations to the affect that may give a clue to its category-triggered origins, in order to examine whether the affect attached to the category is really an appropriate one or one that may need to be reworked. Interestingly, Freud argued that the cathexis of the analyst "will have recourse to *prototypes*, will attach itself to one of the stereotype plates which are present in the subject; or, to put the position in another way, the cathexis will introduce the doctor into one of the physical 'series' which the patient has already formed" (1912, p. 100, emphasis added). Emotions in psychotherapy that can be called transference-related may also arise through the cuing of episodic memories (Tulving 1972) with affects attached. For example, a patient who began coming late to sessions appraised my relatively neutral suggestion that we try to understand the meaning of the lateness during one session as a sadistic expression of rage at her. She associated shortly afterward to a painful memory in which her father beat her for coming home late. In this example a strongly charged memory intervened in her appraisal of my response and produced an inappropriate affective reaction of fear. In this case, however, I had reason to believe that her lateness was a dynamically meaningful repetition of her early experience, so that the memory may have been operative prior to her lateness and involved in producing it.

Transference as Interpersonal Expectancies

People carry with them expectations about what the world holds in store, and these expectations apply not only to the natural world but to the social world as well. Rotter (1966) has emphasized the extent to which we form such expectancies about ourselves, such as internal or external locus of control. Hume argued that as scientists we must make the rationally unfounded assumption that nature will continue to operate much the same tomorrow as it did today, and as intuitive scientists (Ross 1977) we must make a similar assumption if we wish to maintain some sort of order in our lives. Without such an assumption, a scientist could never generalize or predict, and a person could never plan or anticipate. At the interpersonal level, Erikson's (1963) notion of basic trust denotes a similar assumption of the continuity and sameness over time of ourselves and significant others. Without such an assumption, the world of people appears malevolent and capricious, and life is perpetual chaos.

The vignette with which this paper opened portrays rather starkly the phenomenological reality of a woman who lives in such a world, a reality common to many with borderline personality disorders. One can readily see how her encounter with me revealed certain generalized expectancies about what people will do to her. One crucial distinction that is too seldom made in psychoanalytic discussions of transference is between relatively specific and generalized expectancies. Cognitive psychology has for years relied upon hierarchical models of the storage of information within categories and subcategories. One should therefore not be surprised to find interpersonal expectancies ordered in such a fashion, and one could hypothesize that to the extent that such expectancies are more generalized, they will be more recalcitrant to therapeutic change. Unfortunately, such expectancies can also be expected to have the most pervasive impact on interpersonal functioning.

Generalized expectancies of the behavioral responses of social actors form a large category, of which expectancies about men, women, authority figures, and the like form subclasses with more specific expectancies. At the least general level are expectancies related to the behaviors of particular persons in particular situations. Whenever the patient displays an expectation about the therapist, the latter must—within the limitations of admittedly imperfect clinical inference processes (see Turk and Salovey, in press)—attempt to discover the highest-level category to which the expectation applies. The clinician should ideally do this through an hypothesis-testing process that entails looking for

patterns and comparing specific reactions to the therapist with
known reactions of the patient to other people and classes of
people (see Strupp and Binder 1984). While in theory the distinction between levels of expectancy has not been made in psychoanalytic writing on transference, in practice clinicians comment
far less upon reactions to the therapist that appear idiosyncratic
an situation-specific, as compared to those that emerge repeatedly in the patient's life.

Transference as Scripts

Another aspect of transference is the activation of scripts.
Abelson (1981) and Schank and Abelson (1977) have elaborated
the concept of scripts, by which they mean schemas embodying
knowledge of stereotyped event sequences. Scripts permit comprehension of social events and organize action. They often
include expectations of specific sequences of action, and studies
such as Bower and colleagues (1979) and Graesser and colleagues
(1980) provide evidence that people tend to fill in gaps of
knowledge about specific social interactions with stereotyped
scripted knowledge.

Scripts are routinized and do not necessarily require conscious attention. One completes the steps required to dine at a
restaurant, for example, without consciously planning each step
(such as reading the menu). The routinized nature of scripts
renders them likely to be evoked without conscious attention,
and one suspects that, as in the case of other schemas, they will
be activated to the extent that consciously or unconsciously
cognized events or cues match certain features encoded in the
script. This renders likely the elicitation of scripts in psychotherapy that have become routinized in relation to other situations. Numerous scripts may, for example, be activated when in
the presence of an authority, and such scripts are likely to bear
imprints of early authority relationships.

With scripts as with other schemas, the clinician must
attempt to assess the generality or specificity of eliciting condi-

tions. At the broadest level, an individual may have a script for general social interaction and a series of hierarchically arranged subscripts ranging from interaction with women to interaction with mother when confessing a misdeed. Patients frequently recognize the activation of such scripts in therapy, as when a patient spontaneously offered that he was telling me all of his failures and avoiding discussing any triumphs just as he did with his mother, who would commiserate with him about the cruelty of the world but turn icy at any indication of pride. The activation of such scripts is obviously not independent of the evocation of related schemas such as generalized or specific interpersonal expectancies. This particular patient not only behaved toward me as he had toward his mother but expected me to respond as she did, and he was at first angry and surprised when I did not. The script notion can encompass such schemas since it includes knowledge of reciprocal role relations.

Transference as Wishes

In the above example, one should note that the patient may not only have been activating an interactional script but may also have been wishing for a particular type of interaction that he expected to find gratifying. The script notion cannot speak to motivational factors such as the patient's *desire* for me to be like his mother. One of the central aspects of transference described by psychoanalysts and psychodynamic psychotherapists is the activation of archaic wishes that are transferred onto the therapist. The question arises as to whether such phenomena can be usefully examined in relation to information-processing theory and research.

As yet, motivational constructs have not proven easily integrable into information-processing theory. I have previously suggested that certain cognitive-affective structures may be useful in accounting for motivation and in integrating psychodynamic and cognitive-behavioral theories (Westen 1985). One form of these is the *wish*. A wish includes a cognition of a desired state and an anticipated affect associated with attainment of that state. It also includes a cognition of the current status of one's attainment or nonattainment of that state, and an affect arising from the discrepancy between desired and cognized reality. A person can be motivated to act either by the anticipated positive affect associated with attainment of the wish, or by the negative affect arising from the discrepancy between ideal and cognized reality. For example, a patient who has developed an erotic transference has a wish to have sexual contact with her or his therapist. This means that she has formed an affect-laden schema of an end-state or goal and is motivated to reduce the discrepancy between the goal and cognized reality by an aversive affect (e.g., a sense of longing) or by an imagined positive affect (e.g., joy or sexual gratification) if she could achieve her desire. She may achieve this goal in displacement by acting out behaviorally, or she may perform a mental operation, such as fantasizing, to allay her distress or achieve satisfaction. In both cases her action (either behavioral or mental) is motivated by an affect produced by this schema. Every element of this cognitive-affective schema and the responses it evokes (including the affect-laden set-goal, the understanding of reality and expectations of resultant affect if the wish is fulfilled, the discrepancy, and the choice of response to the affect) has a history that is involved in producing the transference experience.

This view of wishes is not incompatible with psychoanalytic drive theory, as recently reformulated by Brenner (1982). Brenner has argued that the concept of "drive" is actually an abstraction or generalization from the empirical observation of wishes. According to Brenner, wishes are the motivating force in mental life, and are primary data in analytic hours. Drives, in contrast, are theoretical constructs derived from these data. A central aspect of Freud's theory of transference is that transference involves the reactivation of old drives or drive derivatives transferred onto the analyst. From the perspective of Brenner's reformulation, this means that transference entails the displacement of archaic wishes onto the therapist.

Psychoanalytic theory is weak in its explanation of why particular wishes will become salient at particular times, or why certain people will become the object of a wish. Freudian psychosexual theory focuses on a biological timetable of unfolding instinctual aims and objects, but this strictly biological developmental view cannot explain why particular wishes of various sorts become associated with specific objects in adulthood. Empirical research is also lacking on conditions for the evocation of wishes, but one has reason to suppose that one way they may be activated is through typical information processing channels, similar to the activation of other schemas (see, e.g., Anderson 1983, Collins and Loftus 1975). A wish may be viewed as a "node" on a semantic network, which can be activated when other associations along the network have been "primed." Wishes that are associatively connected to particular thoughts, feelings, or memories can thus be reawakened if these associated mental events are activated. Further, one may suppose that a wish, like any other schema, is more likely to be elicited to the extent that situational (or intrapsychic) circumstances fit certain prototypical characteristics. In psychotherapy, wishes from previous situations and relationships may thus be evoked, so that the patient desires things from the therapist that she or he desired from significant others. Since the therapy relationship may be one of a small number of relationships with elements that resemble early relationships, the possibility arises that the patient may experience archaic wishes with the therapist that may have been dormant for years.

As with other schemas, one must distinguish between category levels with respect to wishes. Wishes may be quite general (e.g., broad interpersonal wishes such as the desire to be liked) or specific (e.g., the wish for one's father to stay home on one's birthday as a child rather than to travel out of town, to prove his affection). Again, the clinician must attempt to discover the level of generality of wishes experienced toward the therapist and any pattern of their elicitation within and without the therapy situation.

Transference as Defense

Psychoanalytic psychologists argue that not only does transference entail the reenactment of archaic wishes, but that many of these wishes are repressed. One of the greatest stumbling blocks to integration of psychodynamic with information-processing models is that cognitivists and psychodynamic psychologists disagree upon whether one needs to explain certain phenomena with motivational constructs (such as drives and defenses) or whether one can more parsimoniously explain the same phenomena in cognitive terms. Nisbett and Ross (1980), for example, detail a bevy of factors that bias that "intuitive scientist's" understanding of self and others, and they argue for strictly cognitive explanations. Elsewhere (Westen 1985) I have argued that one need not pose the question as information processing versus defense if one synthesizes an understanding of the elicitation and management of affect with information-processing mechanisms. In so doing one can bring together certain aspects of psychodynamic and cognitive-behavioral theory. One can do this by examining what I have called a *cognitive-evaluative mismatch*, of which a wish (as described earlier) is a subtype. The basic notion is derived from systems theory and suggests that an individual establishes a "set-goal" or ideal state with respect to some stimulus or situation, and that a discrepancy or "mismatch" between set-goal and cognized reality produces an affect or feeling. The affect performs a feedback function, activating various control mechanisms designed to minimize the affect.

These control mechanisms may be either behavioral or mental. The function of both is to alleviate the dysphoric affect, and to the extent that a control mechanism is successful, it will be "negatively reinforced" through its association with reduction of a painful emotional state. The behavior or defense mechanism will be encoded as a successful solution and will thus be more likely to be activated upon presentation of a similar situation. If, for example, a child develops death wishes toward a parent and compares these wishes with internalized moral standards, the discrepancy between these standards and cognized reality produces a painful affect, guilt. In order to alleviate the guilt, he may utilize a behavior (acting especially nice to the parent) or a defense (denying his aggressive wishes) or some combination of behavior and defense. In each case he is reducing the cognitive-evaluative mismatch between ideal and cognized reality, either by making reparation or by distorting his self-understanding. The result is a diminution of the guilt and an association of the control mechanism with guilt reduction.

Repeated success with a particular mechanism may result in its automatic elicitation in similar circumstances. Again, in evaluating the use of such mechanisms a therapist must try to pin down the specificity or generality of their use and of the stimuli that elicit them. The notion of cognitive-evaluative mismatch is in many ways similar to Lazarus's (1981) discussion of the processes through which stress activates various coping mechanisms, and Plutchik's (1980) analysis, following Freud, of the utilization of defenses to modulate anxiety.[4]

Freud argued as early as 1912 that transference can be used as a defense or, as defenses are frequently considered in psychoanalysis and psychodynamic psychotherapy, a resistance. (For a comparative analysis of resistance in cognitive-behavioral and psychoanalytic treatment, see Wachtel 1982.) This defensive function of transference must be distinguished from other aspects of the relationship between patient and therapist that are often labeled as transference (such as attachment or erotic interest) because it may operate independently of these other aspects. One defensive use of the transference occurs when a patient focuses upon current features of the relationship with the therapist in order to avoid bringing to awareness painful prototypes of the present situation. Characteristics of the relationship with the therapist may become salient because of their association with affect-laden material, while the thoughts or wishes originally associated with the affect remain repressed. Similarly, the patient

---

[4]See also Haan's (1977) work on coping and defending. I have here provided only an extremely simplified example; elsewhere (Westen 1985) I have developed the model in considerable detail.

may defensively focus on the therapist or the therapeutic relationship to aid in repression of, or selective inattention to, material not related to the therapist. Another defensive use of the transference occurs when the patient distorts his image of the therapist into someone inept or untrustworthy; in so doing he can prevent himself from processing comments or interpretations that are potentially painful or anxiety-provoking.

THERAPEUTIC USES OF TRANSFERENCE

One may thus distinguish seven phenomena that frequently fall under the rubric of transference: person schemas/object representations, attachments, schema-triggered affects, interpersonal expectancies, scripts, wishes, and defenses. If one wishes to speak coherently about transference, it is important to distinguish between these aspects, since the degree to which they or their eliciting events covary is by no means clear.

I will now try to demonstrate the usefulness of working with transference as a therapeutic tool, using convergent data from the laboratory to corroborate the psychodynamic assertion, based on clinical experience, that the use of transference material is therapeutically critical.

The Assessment and Alteration of Scripts, Expectancies, and Wishes

One important use of transference is in the assessment and alteration of scripts, expectancies, and wishes. Transference phenomena allow the therapist to peer beyond the patient's self-reports by demonstrating in vivid detail the way the patient interacts with, and what the patient expects and desires from, significant others (see Strupp and Binder 1984). This is not to imply that clinicians are always successful in assessing the generality of those schemas. Clinical inference is difficult enough when dealing with behaviors, let alone with schemas (especially schemas uncovered through interaction). In this respect, the analysis of transference is a microcosm of social scientific method:

it is at once hermeneutic and positivist. On the one hand, interpretation of transference material is a hermeneutic art, akin to the interpretation of a text because the words and deeds of the patient are likely to function as metaphor. This can be explained by examining the interaction of cognitive and dynamic processes. Since certain thoughts and wishes are connected with painful affects, they are likely to be repressed and thus to remain inaccessible to consciousness. Yet cognitions associated with them may emerge into consciousness (because the repression does not obliterate the entire associational network), or be incorporated into easily assimilable aspects of the therapy situation, such as thoughts about the therapist or events being described in the treatment hour. The result is that the patient communicates in metaphor, and the interpretation of symbols is as difficult in therapeutic discourse as it is in literature. On the other hand, once the therapist begins to suspect the presence of a latent web of associations, he must act like a natural scientist as hypothesis tester, presenting and listening for situations likely to confirm or disconfirm the hypothesis. He may speak to the patient in related metaphor or directly interpret the material and gauge the patient's reactions. In his hypothesis testing he is vulnerable to the same distortions as other "intuitive scientists" (Ross 1977), whose schemas tend to be more robust in assimilating or ignoring discrepant information than they should, but this is a limitation of all science, not just intuitive science or clinical practice.[5]

The relationship between therapist and patient is an invaluable source of information about the patient's interpersonal action schemas (scripts), assumptions about the social world (expectancies), and wishes. As noted earlier, a great deal of research has demonstrated that much of cognitive processing occurs outside of awareness, and decades of clinical work attest to the unconscious "processing" of motives and affects. Indeed, a wealth of

---

[5]Kuhn (1970), in fact, rejected Popper's (1963) view of science as a hypothetico-deductive, hypothesis-testing enterprise precisely because he found, in scrutinizing the history of science, that disconfirming instances only topple a paradigm when they are overwhelming and when an alternative paradigm is in existence.

experimental evidence has recently been adduced to document unconscious emotional processes as well (Westen 1985). Many of these scripts, expectancies, and wishes become routinized and are activated automatically in relevant circumstances. Consequently, if recognized at all, they appear "natural" to the patient, who has been using them for years. The therapist may use such phenomena in the transference not only to learn about the patient's schemas but also to point them out to the patient and thus de-routinize them. By making these schemas explicit and conscious, the therapist can help the patient examine and change them if they appear to be erroneous or maladaptive.

The Uncovering of State-Dependent Memories and Schema-Triggered Affects

Much recent experimental research (Bower 1981, Clark and Teasdale 1982, Derry and Kuiper 1981, Roth and Rehm 1980) has demonstrated the significance of feeling states on memory retrieval. This research has shown that retrieval of affect-laden thoughts or memories is influenced by mood at the time of retrieval. Bower (1981) has applied this to both semantic and episodic memory (Tulving 1972) and has demonstrated the effect of mood on recall of childhood memories. To the extent that the therapeutic situation evokes old schemas, it is likely to activate associated affects, which in turn trigger state-dependent memories. Freud (1917) similarly argued that a central function of transference is that it awakens old conflicts. From a perspective that integrates cognitive and dynamic concepts, a conflict can be understood as the presence of wishes, cognitive-evaluative mismatches, or other cognitive-affective schemas, such that satisfaction of one such motive has a negative influence on another. Satisfaction of an aggressive wish, for example, may simultaneously conflict with an "ideal self" set-goal (or "superego prohibition"), producing a cognitive-evaluative mismatch and consequently a feeling of guilt. As psychoanalytic theory and practice suggests, the response to a conflict of this sort is likely to be a compromise formation.

The utility of triggering such memories, affects, and conflicts is that they may lie at the root of dysfunctional behavior and mental processes. One of the fundamental assumptions of psychoanalytic method (see Rapaport 1944) is that every thought, wish, and fantasy has a history. In Piagetian terms, every schema is the end-product of a series of assimilations and accommodations. A crucial aspect of the schemas determinative of much of human behavior — and of psychopathology — is that they are affective as well as cognitive.

Developmentally, as the cognitive component of a schema changes, associated affects may also change, but in other cases they may not. Similarly, while a new schema may become more prominent in a network of associations and therefore more retrievable, old versions of the schema may continue to influence behavior despite their relative inaccessibility to consciousness. In both cases more primitive affects associated with a cognition may inhibit satisfaction or maintain a dysfunctional behavior. For example, as Freud's psychosexual theory has long made clear, affects attached to sex that are either culturally prescribed or based upon ontogenetically primitive conceptions of sexuality may impede sexual pleasure or behavior. Wishes developed in childhood toward significant others may similarly continue to be operative and may be revealed in the transference. A crucial feature of primitive wishes, conflicts, affective responses, and memories of this sort is that they may become repressed in childhood to avoid dysphoric affect. As a result, they may remain encapsulated in "pockets" of unworked-through cognitive-affective networks and may continue to direct thought and behavior. By bringing these cognitive-affective structures to consciousness, the patient can begin to reassess as an adult whether these structures are realistic and whether the way they were regulated in childhood should continue to operate.[6]

---

[6]Analysis of schema-related affects is central to both psychodynamic and cognitive-behavioral understanding of behavior and psychopathology. For example, with respect to phobias, while the two approaches differ significantly in etiological theories, both presuppose (translating into information-processing terms) that an affect has erro-

Freud (1937) referred to this aspect of the therapeutic process as the replacement of an infantile decision by a more adaptive one. At times, the transference provides the only access to such material, by eliciting affects that recruit relevant memories and wishes. For example, a borderline patient whom I had been seeing for over a year started to withdraw without clear cause, refusing to talk and sitting glumly in her chair. We had previously discussed a similar pattern in her life of suddenly severing relations with people important to her, but the pattern was now emerging—with corresponding affect—in the transference. She was aware of her actions but angrily told me that she would not and could not explain them. I suggested to her that someone does not pull away from another person like that unless she is afraid of something, at which point she volunteered that she did not know what she feared, but that she was sure something terribly bad would happen if she did not run. The combination of her experiencing this feeling with me and eliciting thoughts and memories congruent with the affect allowed us to explore the fear behind her behavior, and repeated experiences of this sort allowed her both to reanalyze (cognitively) conditions under which fear has been inappropriately evoked, and to see that, in fact, her fears are not confirmed in interaction with me. This latter aspect of use of the transference is similar to in vivo exposure techniques in behavioral treatment. Wachtel (1977) has lucidly argued for the importance of exposure to anxiety-provoking thoughts, images, and stimuli in both psychoanalytic and behavioral therapies, proposing that the gradual movement from screen memories and thoughts to more deeply repressed material is, in part, similar to systematic desensitization.

---

neously become attached to a cognitive representation, so that the person is afraid of an innocuous stimulus. Similarly, the person may have developed presently maladaptive self-efficacy and outcome expectancies (Bandura 1977, 1982) at a time in which they may or may not have been appropriate, and bringing these to light can help the person alter his behavior.

The Reworking of Behavioral and Intrapsychic Affect-Regulation Mechanisms

In the above example, one avenue for making inroads on the patient's very problematic object relations was to address her pattern of withdrawing from intimate relationships as a way of reducing her fear. She was afraid both of her own rage and destructiveness and of the motives of anyone who would become close to her, and these fears had roots in her earliest experiences of intimacy and closeness. In order to be of help to someone in a situation such as this, the therapist must first point out the behavior, then link it with the affect, explore the source of the affect (which in this case no longer conforms to reality), and finally either reduce the affect or help the patient develop a more adaptive response. Many of the responses that appear pathological in adults were originally responses to rational or irrational fears earlier in life; the response became routinized in childhood when it was associated with regulation of the aversive affect. One significant aim of treatment is thus, as Freud put it, to make the unconscious conscious: a person cannot alter a behavior of which he is not aware, and he is unlikely even then to change it unless he understands that the function it serves is unnecessary or that a more efficient mechanism may be used in its place.

If this is true of behaviors or scripts that are automatically evoked, it is equally true of intrapsychic processes (defenses and other compromise formations) that fulfill the similar function of regulation of affect. Defenses are more difficult to expose than many behaviors because their efficacy presupposes their inaccessibility to consciousness; repression does not work (i.e., does not alleviate an aversive emotional state) if one is aware that one is repressing. The patient has good reason to avoid awareness of such defenses because their use has been "reinforced" by the elimination of a painful affect. The patient is thus unlikely to be willing to relinquish a defense unless he has come to see that the situation is not so unpleasant or frightening, or that he can respond to it in ways that will not so greatly compromise other motives or produce as much distress.

Examination of transference is especially useful because it allows the therapist directly to observe the behavioral and defensive processes the patient brings to bear, especially in social situations. It also gives the therapist concrete and mutually verifiable evidence of these processes to help the patient recognize them, even when doing so is threatening or painful. In addition, bringing to light conflictual material allows for the emergence of more deeply buried issues that are themselves likely to emerge in the transference, in part sometimes creating what psychoanalysts refer to as the "transference neurosis" (see, e.g., Blum 1971, Weinshel 1971). Further, Freud emphasized the patient's use of transference as resistance, a resistance which, if not interpreted, can frequently lead to termination of treatment. This resistance may emerge whether or not the therapist believes in the concept of transference (see Wachtel 1982).

CONCLUSIONS

A general discussion of the causal agents in therapeutic change is obviously outside the parameters of the article, though the foregoing suggests two crucial avenues for change: the alteration of dysfunctional schemas, and the reworking of behavioral and defensive responses evoked to regulate affect.[7] Both are central to psychodynamic psychotherapy, though the alteration of childhood constructions of reality has received less attention at a theoretical level than motivational and defensive shifts. The theoretical systems underlying cognitive therapies have paid great attention to the (conscious) cognitive processes involved in psychopathology but have not as yet come to integrate an understanding of the dynamic influence of affect and affect-regulation mechanisms on mental and behavioral events. To the extent that the phenomena delineated here as aspects of transfer

---

[7]For a more detailed discussion, particularly as applied to short-term psychodynamic psychotherapy, see Westen (1986).

ence can be useful in the assessment and alteration of schemas and modes of affect-regulation, they provide an important tool for therapeutic change. That the use of a process that enlists the active participation of the patient may be especially efficacious in treatment should not be surprising to cognitive-behavioral clinicians. Behavioral therapists for some time have known that participatory modeling is more efficacious than observational learning, and one would thus expect that activating real feelings, interactional patterns, and schemas in psychotherapy would have greater impact than simply talking about them or observing them at a distance.

One could conclude from all this that Freud was overstating the matter somewhat when he claimed that the transference is the battlefield upon which *all* battles must be fought in psychotherapy (1917). The schemas and affect-regulation mechanisms evoked in therapy are only a subset of the person's repertoire, albeit a subset to which the therapist will have greater access and with which he is more likely to effect lasting change.[8] Nevertheless, while Freud was not entirely correct in asserting, in the passage with which this paper began, that one can never destroy anyone in absentia, he was no doubt brilliantly insightful in his recognition that even a straw man burns faster than a memory.

REFERENCES

Abelson, R. P. (1981). Psychological status of the script concept. *American Psychologist* 36:715–729.
Anderson, J. R. (1983). *The Architecture of Cognition*. Cambridge, MA: Harvard University Press.

---

[8]A tendency to exaggerate the role of transference is not surprising in a therapeutic mode in which the therapist must take such a self-abnegatory stance, utilizing his own feelings only insofar as they provide insight into the patient's conflicts and the interpersonal process. Transference is a way for the therapist to bring himself – even a distorted version thereof – into his work.

Bandura, A. (1977). Self-efficacy: toward a unifying theory of behavioral change. *Psychological Review* 84:191-215.

_____ (1982). Self-efficacy mechanism in human agency. *American Psychologist* 37:122-147.

Bartlett, F. (1932). *Remembering*. New York: Columbia University Press.

Blum, H. P. (1971). On the conception and development of the transference neurosis. *Journal of the American Psychoanalytic Association* 19:41-53.

Bower, G. H. (1981). Mood and memory. *American Psychologist* 36:129-148.

Bower, G. H., Black, J., and Turner, T. (1979). Scripts in text comprehension and memory. *Cognitive Psychology* 11:177-220.

Bowlby, J. (1969, 1973). *Attachment and Loss*. Vols. 1 and 2. New York: Basic Books.

Brenner, C. (1982). *The Mind in Conflict*. New York: International Universities Press.

Breuer, J., and Freud, S. (1895). Studies on hysteria. *Standard Edition* 2.

Cantor, N., and Mischel, W. (1979). Prototypes in person perception. In *Advances in Experimental Social Psychology*, vol. 12, ed. L. Berkowitz. New York: Academic.

Cantor, N., Mischel, W., and Schwartz, J. (1982). A prototype analysis of psychological situations. *Cognitive Psychology* 14:45-77.

Clark, D. M., and Teasdale, J. D. (1982). Diurnal variation in clinical depression and accessibility of memories of positive and negative experiences. *Journal of Abnormal Psychology* 91:87-95.

Collins, A. M., and Loftus, E. S. (1975). A spreading-activation theory of semantic processing. *Psychological Review* 82:407-428.

Derry, P. A., and Kuiper, N. A. (1981). Schematic processing and self-referents in clinical depression. *Journal of Abnormal Psychology* 90:286-297.

Erikson, E. (1963). *Childhood and Society*. New York: W. W. Norton.

Fiske, S. (1982). Schema-triggered affect applications to social perception. In *Affect and Cognition. The 17th annual Carnegie symposium on cognition*, ed. M. S. Clarke and S. T. Fiske. Hillsdale, NJ: Lawrence Erlbaum.

Freud, S. (1895). Studies on hysteria. *Standard Edition* 2:255-305.

_____ (1905). Fragment of an analysis of a case of hysteria. *Standard Edition* 7.

_____ (1912). The dynamics of transference. *Standard Edition* 12:97-108.

_____ (1915). Observations on transference-love. *Standard Edition* 12:159–171.

_____ (1917). *Introductory Lectures on Psychoanalysis*. Lectures XXVII and XXVIII. New York: Norton, 1966.

_____ (1937). Analysis terminable and interminable. In *Collected Papers*, vol. 5, 1950.

Gill, M. (1982). *The Analysis of Transference*. Vol. 1: *Theory and Technique*. New York: International Universities Press.

Graesser, A. C., Woll. S. B., Kowalski, D. J., and Smith, D. A. (1980). Memory for typical and atypical actions in scripted activities. *Journal of Experimental Psychology: Human Learning and Memory* 6:503–515.

Haan, N. (1977). *Coping and Defending: Processes of Self-Environment Organization*. New York: Academic.

Holt, R. (1976). Drive or wish? A reconsideration of the psychoanalytic theory of motivation. In *Psychology Versus Metapsychology. Psychoanalytic Essays in Memory of George S. Klein*, ed. M. Gill and P. Holzman. *Psychological Issues Monograph 36*, 9, No. 4, 158–197.

Kuhn, T. S. (1970). *The Structure of Scientific Revolutions*. 2nd ed. Chicago: University of Chicago Press.

Landau, R. J., and Goldfried, M. R. (1981). The assessment of schemata: a unifying framework for cognitive, behavioral, and traditional assessment. In *Assessment Strategies for Cognitive-Behavioral Interventions*, ed. P. C. Kendall and S. D. Hollon. New York: Academic.

Lazarus, R. (1981). The stress and coping paradigm. In *Models for Clinical Psychopathology*, ed. C. Eisdorfer, D. Cohen, A. Kleinman, and P. Maxim, New York: Spectrum.

Markus, H. (1977). Self-schemata and processing information about the self. *JPSP* 35:63–78.

Nisbett, R. E., and Ross, C. (1980). *Human Inference Strategies and Shortcomings of Social Judgment*. Englewood Cliffs, NJ: Prentice-Hall.

Nisbett, R. E., and Wilson, T. D. (1977). Telling more than we can know: verbal reports on mental processes. *Psychological Review* 84:231–259.

Piaget, J. (1926). *The Language and Thought of the Child*. New York: Harcourt Brace.

Plutchik, R. (1980). A general psychoevolutionary theory of emotion. In

Emotion Theory, Research and Experience, ed. R. Plutchik and H. Kellerman. New York: Academic.

Popper, K. (1963). *Conjectures and Refutations*. London: Routledge.

Rapaport, D. (1944). The scientific methodology of psychoanalysis. In *Collected Papers of David Rapaport*. New York: Basic Books, 1967.

Ross, L. (1977). The intuitive psychologist and his shortcomings. In *Advances in Experimental Social Psychology*, vol. 10, ed. L. Berkowitz. New York: Academic.

Roth, D., and Rehm, L. P. (1980). Relationships among self-monitoring processes, memory, and depression. *Cognitive Therapy and Research* 4:149–158.

Rotter, J. B. (1966). Generalized expectancies for internal versus external control of reinforcement. *Psychological Monographs* 80, Whole No. 609.

Schank, R. C., and Abelson, R. P. (1977). *Scripts, Plans, Goals, and Understanding*. Hillsdale, NJ: Lawrence Erlbaum.

Shantz, C. U. (1983). Social cognition. In *Handbook of Child Psychology*. Vol. 3: *Cognitive Development*, ed. P. Mussen. New York: Wiley.

Shevrin, H., and Dickman, S. (1980). The psychological unconscious: a necessary assumption for all psychological theory? *American Psychologist* 35:421–434.

Singer, J. L. (1985). Transference and the human condition: a cognitive-affective perspective. *Psychoanalytic Psychology* 2:189–219.

Sroufe, L., and Waters, E. (1979). Attachment as an organizational construct. *Child Development* 48:1184–1199.

Strupp, H. H., and Binder, J. L. (1984). *Psychotherapy in a New Key: A Guide to Time-Limited Dynamic Psychotherapy*. New York: Basic Books.

Taylor, S. E., and Crocker, J. (1980). Schematic bases of social information processing. In *Social Cognition: the Ontario Symposium*, ed. E. T. Higgins, P. M. Herman, and M. P. Zanna. Hillsdale, NJ: Lawrence Erlbaum.

Tulving, E. (1972). Episodic and semantic memory. In *Organization of Memory*, ed. E. Tulving and W. Donaldson. New York: Academic.

Turk, D. C., and Salovey, P. (in press). Cognitive structures, cognitive processes, and cognitive-behavior modification: I. Client issues. *Cognitive Therapy Research*.

Wachtel, P. L. (1977). *Psychoanalysis and Behavior Therapy: Toward an Integration*. New York: Basic Books.

_____ (1981). Transference, schema, and assimilation: the relationship of Piaget to the psychoanalytic theory of transference. *Annual of Psychoanalysis* 8:59–76.

_____ (1982). *Resistance: Psychodynamic and Behavioral Approaches.* New York: Plenum.

Weinshel, E. M. (1971). The transference neurosis: a survey of the literature. *Journal of the American Psychoanalytic Association* 19:67–88.

Westen, D. (1985). *Self and Society: Narcissism, Collectivism, and the Development of Morals.* Cambridge, England: Cambridge University Press.

_____ (1986). What changes in short-term psychodynamic psychotherapy? *Psychotherapy.*

Zajonc, R. (1968). Attitudinal effects of mere exposure. *Journal of Personality and Social Psychology Monographs* vol. 9.

3

Learning Theory and Psychoanalysis[1]

Eugene Wolf

EDITOR'S SYNOPSIS

This paper was selected for its lucid description of the development and maintenance of impaired interpersonal relations, and for its suggestions as to how such behavior may be unlearned with the therapist. Writing from a social learning perspective, Wolf provides very apt operational descriptions of transference, and how it may be used to create change. Of particular importance to here-and-now transference analysis is his observation that patients will attempt to induce the therapist to behave in an expected manner that supports their maladaptive functioning. The therapist is helpful to the degree he is able to control his reactions, avoid the "expected" response, and instead provide a corrective response. While not going into depth on what a corrective response entails, Wolf sensitizes the therapist to the

[1]This paper was published in *British Journal of Medical Psychology*, 1966; 39:1–10.

importance of careful attention to the patient–therapist interaction. Of additional importance is his view that change is most effectively accomplished when the patient is involved in a "first-hand experience" engaging his emotions as well as intellect.

At a time when cybernetics has come to relate the behavior of man to that of lifeless machines, we cannot possibly turn our backs on the model of something as close to man as is another mammal. The animal model is, however, a potentially double-edged weapon. It can be a blessing to the extent to which we succeed in establishing all that man and animal have in common, but it can also prove to be a hindrance to the extent to which we fail to establish the relevant features in which the two differ at the same time.

PERSISTENCE OF MALADAPTIVE BEHAVIOR

It is a characteristic feature of ontogenetic and even of phylogenetic learning that responses, or systems of responses, that are no longer adaptive and enhancing the needs of the organism tend to be shed and discarded. In the absence of constancy of living conditions, the maintenance of life of individuals as well as species is dependent on their flexible adaptivity, which consists as much in their capacity to extinguish and abandon patterns of behavior that are no longer appropriate to the changed conditions as in their capacity to acquire and retain new appropriate ones. All this is in full keeping with the reward–punishment model of learning: adaptive behavior being reinforced by its own rewarding outcome is retained, whereas unadaptive behavior that cannot be reinforced by its own harmful outcome is cast off and extinguished.

In applying this "instrumental" (operant) model of learning to human psychopathology, we come up against the disconcerting paradox that maladaptive patterns in man, once acquired, may be retained for years in spite of their repeatedly *unrewarding and even incapacitating outcome.* Learning theorists have put forward a number of attempts to explain this contradiction. One way of accounting for the persistence of a pathological pattern, such as a phobia, is that it is essentially an avoidance response to a feared stimulus or situation. Even though it is not appropriate or no longer appropriate, by avoiding the stimulus the organism deprives itself also of further opportunities to unlearn what may be, or may have already become, an inappropriate response (Eysenck 1960). But if avoidance behavior is designed to avoid suffering, how can this apply to mental patients? Is a psychogenic disorder designed to avoid suffering, or is it suffering itself? If the disorder really protects the patient from suffering, why call any kind of procedure that deprives him of such protection "therapeutic"?

In the avoidance hypothesis the persistence of the morbid pattern is ascribed to absence of reexposure, that is, absent opportunities not only for further reinforcements but also for extinction through nonreinforcement. A more commonly put forward explanation is that maladaptive patterns persist because they *are* being constantly reinforced by their own rewarding outcomes. The reinforcing reward may be a negative one, such as repeatedly experienced relief from fear, but the rewarding outcome may also be a positively pleasurable one. But in either case is this not a contradiction in terms? Why call a pattern that is rewarding to the organism "maladaptive"? And why cure patients of patterns that are beneficial to them?

All forms of mental and bodily sickness may be to some extent compensated for by the various allowances made by society for the temporarily or permanently disabled. It is also an indisputable clinical fact that under certain circumstances a psychogenic illness may prove to be the lesser of two or more alternative evils available to the patient. But by being a lesser evil, *illness as a whole never ceases to be an evil* in its consequences for the patient. Whatever the secondary and partial gains accruing from illness may be, it would be scientifically untenable to argue that mental ill-health, with the concomitant suffering and limitations to effective living, can ever *outweigh motivationally* mental health in the *totality* of satisfactions. If this were the case, patients would never ask to be relieved of their illness and it would become altogether debatable how far pathological behavior is at all maladaptive.

From the point of view of learning and motivation, what else can the rationale underlying aversion therapy imply but that the illness to be erased by it is either pleasurable to the patient, or at least less unpleasurable than is a series of induced vomiting or some other disagreeable procedure? Treatment by punishment is, of course, no novelty in the history of our discipline. Though in former ages it was not meted out with methodological precision, some may think that the demonological rationale was perhaps more logical.

A PSYCHODYNAMIC MODEL OF LEARNING

The psychodynamic model of learning presented in this discussion leans in its general outlines on Sullivan's (1955) interpersonal theory of psychopathology, on Alexander and French's (1946) formulation of the transference in terms of generalization and on their concept of the "corrective emotional experience" to which the patient is exposed in the therapeutic relationship, and on Masserman's (1946) concept of conflict behavior.

In the model put forward here it is assumed that underlying the mental and bodily symptomatology of a psychogenic disorder is a breakdown in adaptive *interpersonal behavior*. An individual's characteristic patterns of behavior to other people, as much as to objects, are learned principally during the formative years of childhood in the course of interactions with significant members of the nuclear family. The interpersonal patterns thus acquired are, with greater or lesser modifications, transferred by way of social generalization into relationships with comparable, equivalent, or derivative human figures. Maladaptive patterns acquired in earlier traumatic relationships may continue manifestly into adulthood in the form of personality anomalies, or may, in the course of subsequent corrective experiences, undergo repair. Such repair may be from a clinical point of view more or less complete or only superficial and tenuous. A precariously integrated system of interpersonal behavior constitutes a latently predisposed personality structure that may break down and decompensate under precipitating stress in later life, and the individual may, as a result, revert (regress) to earlier patterns of immature behavior.

The survival and persistence of typical interpersonal patterns and their carryover into successive relationships of the same category (intimacy, authority, peers) is the recurrent theme of psychiatric case histories, and has been referred to by Freud under such terms as *repetition-compulsion* and *neurosis of destiny*. Pathological patterns of interpersonal behavior are maladaptive to the extent to which they come to be transferred rigidly into new relationships that are only similar but in which they are no longer appropriate. The morbidly *extended gradient of social generalization*, whereby patterns of behavior are promptly and indiscriminately elicited in the patient by human figures only remotely resembling earlier ones, is a measure of the severity of the traumatic interpersonal experiences to which he was previously exposed and in the course of which the patterns were originally acquired. That the gradient of stimulus generalization is a function of the severity of the previous trauma has been experimentally demonstrated in both animal and man (Hilgard and Marquis 1961), and its primary function is apparently defensive. The greater the risk to the organism, the more widespread are the precautions taken against the danger of repetition, as if the organism were "once bitten–twice shy" not only with identical stimuli, but also with similar stimuli. Pathological social generalization by a child or adult, affecting certain interpersonal relationships, may be thought of in psychological terms as a form of impelling "prejudice" against human figures of a certain category. Patterns of response acquired in relation to an excessively authoritarian father, for instance, are maladaptive when they are compulsively and indiscriminately elicited by other subsequent figures in authority, irrespective of how closely the new figures resemble the father's own personality in fact. Patterns of this sort, when displayed by the patient towards the therapist, Freud called "transference."

From his first observations of transference phenomena in the early nineties of the last century, it took Freud (1946a) nearly twenty years to discover and describe the " 'countertransference' which arises in the physician as a result of the patient's influence . . . ," requiring him to recognize it in himself and to overcome it if the patient is to be changed at all. According to Freud (1946b): "It must not be supposed, however, that the transference is created by analysis and does not occur apart from it. Transference is merely uncovered and isolated by analysis. It is a universal phenomenon . . . and in fact dominates the whole of each person's relations to his human environment." This universality of the transference he was able to establish from his patients' own accounts of their repetitive life stories. However, the phenomenon of the countertransference he was only able to identify in himself, for the simple reason that the therapeutic situation was his only available opportunity to investigate *both ends* of a relationship of the patient. Had the rules of psychoanalytic technique not precluded Freud's access to independent environmental data, it would not have taken him long to note that the countertransference was no less ubiquitous than the transference itself. Countertransferences roused by the individual in the lay environment tend to be equally spontaneous and not understood, and to have no modifying impact on the transferential patterns. Lay countertransferences are of no theoretical or practical consequence as far as the psychoanalytic model itself is concerned, but in the model of psychodynamic learning submitted in this discussion it constitutes an indispensable link of interaction and interpersonal feedback.

PERSISTENCE OF INTERPERSONAL PATTERNS

With the exception of early life, no new human relationship is ever initiated at the moment of encounter right from scratch. Into newly opened relationships man always carries over experiences and modes of conduct acquired in previous similar relationships, and this represents his own share in the common undertaking. We could never benefit from previous life experiences if we did not ubiquitously indulge in a normal degree of interpersonal generalization. Even when a patient comes to see us for the first time his initial behavior is less determined by our own conduct than by that of our colleagues whom he had seen before us. If *they* happened to be unduly impatient with him, we should not be surprised to find him distrustful and unconfiding with us too. Since the examination of an uncommunicative patient, especially when the available time is limited, may be a severe test of endurance even for a trained psychiatrist, we should not be surprised if our oversensitive patient does not fail to note *our* inner sighs of despair also. This will naturally only confirm his preconceived assumption that we and our colleagues are much the same kind of people. Having thus failed our patient's test means, unfortunately, that we too have, in our turn, succeeded in perpetuating his uncommunicativeness. What is more, our own responses have, at the same time, predetermined the despair of the psychiatrist who is destined to examine him after us. If we may find a patient to be rather exasperating in one single interview, how much nonreinforcing tolerance can be expected from lay associates who work or even live with him day in and day out?

If an hysterical, psychopathic, or paranoid patient is today still like he was yesterday, this is due to the fact that once again he has succeeded in compelling his environment to "repay him in kind." If the environment is mentally "normal" in that it responds appropriately, once again it will drive him hysterical, psychopathic, or paranoid, as the case may be. It is extremely difficult even to refrain from the patronizing responses that the emotionally immature and dependent patient is consistently drawing from his environment. The element of reinforcing condescension usually implicit in such protective responses will, of course, only continue to bar him from rising to maturity and independence.

Relatives and associates will readily provide us with vivid

accounts of how very difficult and trying it is to respond to a patient differently from what is appropriate to his own conduct. And this is precisely what we are supposed to do in psychotherapy: unlike the natural environment of the patient we are to behave and respond inappropriately and, therefore, "abnormally." Ours is the arduous task of behaving and responding to the patient not according to what he actually is, but what he is not, that is to say, according to what we would like him to be. For as long as the surrounding world of the functional psychotic continues to treat him as a madman, psychotic he is doomed to remain. The same, of course, goes not only for antisocial criminals and neurotics, but for all of us. We all persist in being whatever we are as a result of the fact that we continually succeed in compelling our environments to respond to each one of us in the very particular way in which they actually do.

It is a measure of Freud's genius to have discovered that the extent to which we can at all prove helpful to a patient, is a function of our capacity to control our own responses to him. We are often unaware of subtle metacommunications whereby we give away to our patients the reactions that they compulsively rouse in us. Parents, even if they know that they should strive to behave to their disturbed child not according to what he actually is but according to what they would like him to be, find it very difficult to observe this rule consistently. Yet this, fortunately, is only a general tendency, not a rigid law. We are all familiar with the abrupt and sometimes dramatic changes that may take place in the attitude of the environment to a person who has suffered a breakdown. The homeostatic effect of the various allowances made by the human environment following his admission to hospital, or even mere acceptance into outpatient medical care, is fairly well known. Even the law, and society in general, take a different view of crimes committed by the mentally ill offender, and waive the usual rule of making the punishing response fit the crime.

Investigations of both ends of a patient's extratherapeutic relationships show that, once afflicted by maladaptive patterns, the patient becomes himself an indirect source and a carrier of repeated self-injury mediated by the retaliatory properties of the equally sensitive human environment. He tends to contaminate each new and as yet unbiased relationship with a carryover of morbid patterns acquired in comparable former relationships. By compulsively recreating his earlier interpersonal relationships and situations, *he also tends to reproduce the traumatizing features of his previous environments* only to keep him confirmed in his illness. It may even be illusory to imagine that when we fail to cure a patient, we merely fail to do him any good by way of omission. Are we really justified in assuming that there is no appreciable difference between a psychogenic illness that remains unchanged in the absence of any treatment, and an illness that remains unchanged following unsuccessful therapeutic intervention? Could it not be argued that in his relationship to us we have inevitably confirmed the patient's problems, making our next colleague's task one grade more difficult?

THE PSYCHOTHERAPEUTIC PROCESS

To say that interpersonal dynamics are at play in the persistence of maladaptive behavior does not imply that the disorder could spontaneously fade away following a period of social seclusion and protection from reinforcing environmental traumata. Extinction of a response to a certain stimulus is not the same as forgetting the stimulus altogether. On the contrary, extinction implies the obliteration of the response in any further encounter with the same stimulus. If an impotent patient keeps away from women, true, his difficulties may not be clearly manifest. But treatment means to abolish this inhibitory response whenever he is reexposed to the same, or the same kind of, erotic relationship. The concepts of reinforcement and nonreinforcement are meaningless unless they coincide with reexposure to the conditioned stimulus or situation. An experimentally established salivary response cannot be extinguished by failing to sound the bell altogether, but by repeatedly sounding the bell and yet failing to reinforce the exhibited response.

Nonreinforcement in psychogenic disorders, too, can prove therapeutic only if it is coupled with reexposure to certain interpersonal situations. However, reexposure to the original traumatic relationship is no more essential for abolishing the patterns than it is for perpetuating them. A comparable interpersonal situation with analogous significance, such as the therapeutic relationship, may prove sufficiently effective and corrective for this purpose. The almost instantaneous reexposure of the experimental animal to physical stimuli can bear no comparison in complexity with the laborious psychological reexposure of the patient in the therapeutic situation.

The patient's interpersonal generalizations are bound to envelop also the therapist, and from him, too, the patient will tend to draw and extract countertransferential responses. As Freud says, it is only to the extent to which the therapist will prove capable of differentiating himself in the patient's own experience from previous human figures that the inappropriate and disabling patterns can be surrendered and no longer exhibited in further interpersonal encounters.

FIRST-HAND AND SECOND-HAND LEARNING

We can benefit from experimental psychology only if the relevant dissimilarities as well as the similarities between animal and human learning are borne in mind. There is no valid reason why the behavior of a person in response to the verbal and nonverbal stimuli emitted by another person could not be fitted into a behavioral stimulus–response scheme, with the interposed central processes constituting a Tolmanian intervening variable. The obvious advantage of such a behavioral scheme lies in the fact that, quite independently of intrapsychic processes, the testing of psychodynamic hypotheses can be confined to observable data. In principle, interpersonal behavior in dyadic relationships is not only observable, but also measurable (Wolf et al. 1964). It is perfectly feasible that with the aid of adequate methods it should be possible to investigate, in both longitudinal and transverse studies, not only the relationship of psychogenic symptoms to maladaptive interpersonal behavior, but also such processes as the development and vicissitudes of interpersonal patterns or the universality of transference phenomena (Wolf 1966).

It would be fallacious to expect that the methodological approach involved in the investigation of animal behavior is equally adequate to all aspects of human behavior. The behavior of a laboratory animal may be a subject of direct observation by nonparticipant observers. It does not follow, however, that a laboratory setting that even in the human adult has proved suitable for investigating his characteristic responses to objects and tests, is equally suitable for investigating his characteristic responses to other people. Unlike the prompt responses that may be elicited in animals and infants to pleasant and unpleasant stimuli, an interpersonal response may take days, months, or even years to materialize, as may be the case in acts of retaliation. However, the prolonged latencies with which man often responds, especially to people he significantly depends upon, are not the only reason why interpersonal behavior is unsuited for observation within the confines of limited time and space. Another reason is that one could not possibly accept, say, the behavior of a parent to his child as observed in the setting of a clinic to be a representative sample of his overall behavior to the child at home.

The sole function of learning is to benefit from previous relevant experience, and this much is undoubtedly common to both man and animal. That is why man, when not impulsive and whether investigators like it or not, is a thinking creature who before finally deciding how to respond to a significant person's act, often prefers to take his time and weigh such an act in the light of his previous interpersonal experiences. But this is not the most fundamental difference between human and infrahuman learning. For, unlike the animal who is only capable of profiting from its own experiences that it has itself been exposed to, man, by virtue of his capacities to communicate verbally, can, in addition, also profit from the personal experiences of other people, such as parents or friends. He may decide to consult the latter before finally responding to the other person whom he, say, contemplates divorcing. But this is by no means all, for he may, as an alternative or additional *intermediary response* consult a book on this particular subject or perhaps a psychiatrist, with the aim of profiting from the combined and pooled experiences of many more contemporaries and even past generations, registered in both the book and the psychiatrist's erudition not as verbatim accounts of innumerable life histories but in a generalized and abstracted form of perhaps some psychodynamic theory of marital problems.

That there is a fundamental difference between the therapeutic benefit derived from first-hand experiences and second-hand ones was empirically established by Freud. Not being behaviorally oriented he could only conceptualize the contrast between them in the traditional language of subjective psychology as "emotional" versus "rational" reeducation. In his latest formulation of the therapeutic process Freud laid all the emphasis on the "emotional" experience attained with the aid of concrete interpretations, as against the inefficacy of abstract "intellectual" insight imparted to the patient.

Only what a child or adult has learned from second-hand sources is susceptible to correction or even denial by second-hand as well as first-hand revelations. However, knowledge or lessons drawn from other people's experiences have no corrective capacity if they run counter to the patient's own first-hand experiences. A psychogenic disorder that has grown out of his own interpersonal experiences can be unlearned only by exposing him to new disconfirming first-hand experiences. By sheer force of logical argument we could not possibly convince an antisocial psychopath, who was not only a subject of parental hostility but also of repeated imprisonments and social ostracism, that society or some people are really well disposed to him and want to help him. For what he knows from first-hand experience to have been true for certain, in the course of his therapeutic reeducation he requires to see for himself not that it was not true, but that it is no longer true. He should be offered experiential opportunities to discover for himself that in the therapeutic situation his behavior is anachronistic and no longer appropriate. This is in essence the analysis of the transference.

Maladaptive interpersonal patterns can be unlearned only in face-to-face situations that the patient has a compulsive need to subject to empirical testing to see if they are any different from previous traumatic ones. Such testing is only feasible if there are opportunities to evoke invalidating social feedback (Wolf 1957, 1960). Information conveyed by some impersonal route such as a book or a public lecture, through which in the last analysis innumerable anonymous sufferers and ex-sufferers are addressing their pooled and abstracted experiences to the patient, may be highly instructive but not curative. Recognition of this fact is nowadays implicit in every variety of psychotherapeutic procedure in which face-to-face social encounters with therapist, staff members, and fellow patients are considered indispensable.

CONCLUSION

We should allow ourselves neither to be carried away by the animal model too literally nor to be driven by the complexities of social behavior to the other extreme. What we require is not a behavioral animal model to copy, but a behavioral approach to apply in psychiatric thinking and practice. In a fruitful cooperative spirit the clinician stands as much to gain from the learning theories based on the animal model as does the learning theorist stand to gain from the empirically established principles of learning and unlearning pathological behavior that only pertain to man but have no direct counterpart in the animal.

The learning theory model and the psychoanalytic model are by no means incompatible alternatives. On the contrary, they bear out each other's most important contributions, and interdisciplinary integration of the two models is likely to open up sharper insights into the genesis and treatment of psychogenic disorders. I submit that their integration is sooner or later inevitable, however passionately some or many of us may choose to resist it. Psychoanalysis cannot remain for much longer outside the behavioral sciences, nor can the science of human behavior for much longer ignore the body of knowledge amassed by the psychoanalytic schools of thought.

REFERENCES

Alexander, F., and French, T. M. (1946). *Psychoanalytic Therapy*. New York: Ronald.

Eysenck, H. J. (1960). Personality and behaviour therapy. *Proc. R. Soc. Med.* 53:504–508.

Freud, S. (1946a). *Collected Papers*. 4th ed. Vol. 2. London: Hogarth.

_____ (1946b). *An Autobiographical Study*. 2nd ed. London: Hogarth.

Hilgard, E. R., and Marquis, D. G. (1961). *Conditioning and Learning*. Rev. ed. London: Methuen.

Masserman, J. H. (1946). *Principles of Dynamic Psychiatry*. Philadelphia: Saunders.

Sullivan, H. S. (1955). *Conceptions of Modern Psychiatry*. London: Tavistock.

Wolf, E. (1957). *Congress Report, 2nd Int. Congr. Psychiatry*. Vol. 3. Ed. W. A. Stoll. Zurich: Orell Fuessli.

_____ (1960). *Progress in Psychotherapy*. Vol. 5. Ed. J. H. Masserman and J. L. Moreno. New York: Grune & Stratton.

_____ (1966). Psychogenic disorders and interpersonal behaviour. *J. Psychosom. Res.*

Wolf, E., Dytrych, Z., Grof, S., et al. (1964). A methodological approach to social maladaptation. Mutual social perception inventory. *Cs. Psychiat.* 60:34–37.

4

Patterns of Influence in the Analytic Relationship[1]

Paul L. Wachtel

EDITOR'S SYNOPSIS

This paper was chosen for Wachtel's provocative critique of neutrality explored against the backdrop of his view of personality functioning and change. Wachtel cautions against a rigid adherence to neutrality, fearing that it may compromise the therapist's ability to examine conflicted interpersonal patterns as they are played out within the therapy. Traditionally viewed, the therapist's neutral stance is meant to avoid unduly influencing the patient's transference reaction. A corollary to this view is that the patient responds to all or most therapists in a similar manner, and that his response is determined by what is brought to the encounter rather than the encounter itself. Wachtel disputes this, arguing that a person's individuality is not something stored to emerge if the therapist stays out of the way. Invoking

[1]This paper was published in *Contemporary Psychoanalysis*, 1986; 22(1):60–70.

the work of H. S. Sullivan, Wachtel points out that the therapist cannot avoid influencing what is being observed and that he is always observing behavior that occurs in relation to his presence. Failure to consider this contributes to a skewed view of the interaction and faulty work with transference.

Wachtel stresses repetitive interactive cycles in his view of personality functioning. Conflicted interaction patterns are viewed as deriving from early developmental experience, but being sustained by enlisting present day "accomplices," that is, through inducing others to behave in ways that keep maladaptive patterns alive. Wachtel feels it is essential for patients to see how this is done; it is often the patients' unawareness of how they re-create problems that prompts them to seek therapy in the first place. Wachtel advocates going beyond therapist use of personal reactions as private clues to what is going on in the patient. The therapist's willingness to discuss his experience of the patient is seen as essential in helping the patient better understand himself and how he forms relationships. A neutral stance is deemed problematic if it excludes discussion of what transpires between patient and therapist, particularly if the therapist avoids sharing reactions to the patient.

Proponents of neutrality hold that such a stance is necessary for creation of an "atmosphere of safety." This atmosphere is seen to facilitate patient disclosure and exploration of conflict. Wachtel, however, contends that a neutral stance, including refraining from overt opinions, may actually decrease the patient's sense of safety. Lack of feedback may stimulate patient anxiety resulting in inhibition and decreased willingness to communicate. While this anxiety may be explored, such work does not always lead to an increase in patient willingness to self-disclose. Lack of feedback from the therapist may also make it difficult for the patient to sharpen his ability to assess the emotions of others. This especially may be the case where the patient perceives something and the therapist (under the auspices of neutrality, and often replicating an early experience of the patient with a parent) denies its validity or refuses to discuss it. It is important to note that Wachtel does not advise complete self-disclosure. This is viewed as irresponsible. What is stressed is its judicious use when the therapist feels it would be helpful to the process of clarifying the interpersonal patterns of the patient. In so doing Wachtel seeks to free up the therapist to more actively use himself as a tool for increased insight and change.

Wachtel's arguments are stimulating and presented in a clear and reader-friendly fashion. His emphasis on an active, give-and-take interchange is critical to here-and-now transference analysis. While his conclusions regarding neutrality may not be completely shared, his ideas provide ample food for thought.

The therapeutic stance that is referred to as neutral is designed to protect the patient and the therapeutic situation. It is an effort to structure into the therapeutic process a nonjudgmental frame of mind. It is also an epistemological stance, one designed to permit "deep" material to come forth undistorted by the analyst's input. It is certainly true that our own reactions as analysts or therapists can be problematic. I sympathize with the aims that have led to the precept of neutrality. But I believe that the ideas and practices associated with so-called neutrality are deeply flawed and that we would do well to relinquish our ties to that particular attempted solution to the hazards of doing psychoanalytic therapy.

My dissatisfactions with the idea of neutrality derive largely from Sullivan's implicit recasting of the central premises of psychoanalytic thought. Indeed it is remarkable to me that so many decades after Sullivan—and after Heisenberg—we should still find neutrality so prominently discussed among analysts.

The stance of neutrality is designed to assure that we do not muddy the waters of transference or, to use another commonly used and related metaphor, that we do not contaminate the field. But Sullivan made it clear that one cannot stay outside the field, one cannot avoid influencing what one is observing. We are always observing something that occurs in relation to us, and not just to us as screens or phantoms, but to us as specific flesh and blood human beings sitting in the consulting room.

To be sure, what transpires does not only have to with the

person of the analyst. Some of what the patient experiences he would likely experience in similar fashion whoever was sitting in our chair; and any particular analyst certainly evokes different reactions in different patients. It is essential that the analyst address the unique individuality of the patient (and it is unfortunate that Sullivan, in countering the prevailing atomistic bias of his time, was moved to rhetorical excesses that seemed to some to link his systematic ideas to a denial of individuality). But the person's individuality is not something stored up inside him that just "emerges" or "unfolds" if the analyst just gets out of the way (Wachtel 1982). Rather, we express and exhibit our individuality as living, responsive beings, assimilating new experiences to old psychological structures, and also (inevitably) accommodating those structures to the ongoing events of our lives (Wachtel 1981). We exist and give meaning to our lives in relation to the significant events of our lives.

How long will it take us to be clear that if we are silent we see one aspect of the patient and if we criticize, praise, give advice, laugh at a joke (or don't) we see other, equally significant aspects? As family therapists are fond of saying, one can never "not communicate." The effort to do so is itself a communication—indeed, a very powerful one.

Such arguments have by now become familiar enough that few analysts really claim to be neutral in any thoroughgoing sense. Usually the influence of the analyst is recognized and acknowledged by advocates of neutrality, but the claim is made that one can and should strive to minimize that influence as much as possible. Thus while strict neutrality is admitted to be impossible, relative neutrality is put forth as a valid and salutary ideal. This seemingly sophisticated and realistic position seems to me much like describing someone as a little bit pregnant. Neutrality is not something you can be a little bit of or a lot. It involves a basic epistemological stance: One either recognizes the contextual nature of what one observes in analysis and understands that it is inevitably a product of both live organisms in the room, or one contends that even if one slips some of the time, when one does not slip one has removed oneself from the picture. This latter position does not make sense to me.

Although one cannot be neutral in any epistemologically sensible way, one can certainly behave in the ways that have traditionally been associated with neutrality. One can, for example, be silent much of the time, or titrate the overt expression of one's reactions to the patient. But relative silence is not the same as relative neutrality. Relative silence per se does not imply an epistemological position. It is a way of acting, an interpersonal tactic. Sometimes such a way of interacting with the patient has a useful impact on the therapeutic process (it always has some impact). But its value is limited and often can be counterproductive.

The reason for the limitations of the interactional stance usually assumed by proponents of neutrality again goes back to Sullivan, at least indirectly. Implicit in an interpersonal point of view, I believe, is a vision of personality that stresses repetitive circular processes or interaction cycles (Wachtel 1977b, 1982). The difficulties the patient finds himself in are not simply the product of early experiences, or defensive efforts that have achieved some sort of structuralization. The patient requires "accomplices" to maintain his neurosis (Wachtel 1977a). Without the continuing participation of other people, the pattern cannot sustain itself. Therefore it is essential to understand how the patient induces others to act in ways that keep the maladaptive pattern going. It is essential that the patient understand this too. Self-knowledge, from an interpersonal perspective, is knowledge not just of one's warded off wishes, thoughts, and feelings, but of the interpersonal situations that give rise to such psychological events. It includes understanding the impact that particular interactions have on one's own psychological state, and one's impact on others (which in turn feeds back, through their behavior in relation to oneself, to affect one's own sense of self, usually in a way that again keeps the entire pattern going).

Given such a view, it is easy to see why the stance usually associated with neutrality is unsatisfactory. What one wants the patient to understand in relation to the analyst is not simply that he has seen the analyst incorrectly as resembling an important figure from the past (an aim for which it can be useful for the analyst to appear to have done nothing to merit the patient's attribution). Rather, one wants to use the transference in a different way: as an exemplification of the way the patient sets up a relationship in such a fashion that old patterns are actually repeated. From such a perspective, it is to be expected that the analyst will in fact act like significant figures from the patient's past (and, if the pattern is really one worthy of therapeutic attention, from the patient's present as well). It is to be hoped that the analyst will not participate as an "accomplice" in quite the way that others in the patient's life do; that would hardly be an improvement. But even if the analyst's participation is more modulated, modified by his being a participant observer, it is almost inevitable that he will in some way replicate the experience others have with the patient (cf. Wolf 1966). But this is not as unfortunate as it may sound at first. For it is in the very act of participating that the analyst learns what it is most important to know about the patient. And it is in coming to see their joint participation in what is for him a familiar pattern, but a joint participation with the crucial difference of reflectiveness, that the patient too learns what he must in order to begin the process of change.

If the analyst adopts the pose of neutrality, this crucial aspect of therapeutically useful insight is short-circuited. It is precisely in pointing out how the patient's reactions are not simply a distortion, in examining just how the patient has evoked a familiar reaction (first internal, then overt) from the analyst, that the most therapeutically valuable aspect of the work is achieved (cf. Epstein and Feiner 1979, Gill 1979).

The virtue of the analytic interaction lies in how it replicates and deviates from other significant interactions in the patient's life. Such a combination of replication and deviation need not be approached in an artificial or manipulative way. It happens inevitably, whether one intends it or not. The force field of the patient's emotional pull on the one hand, and the effects of training and self-reflection on the other, see to that.

The replication aspect, of course, is not likely to be immediately fully recognized by the patient. Part of why he is in analysis is precisely because he does not see how he brings about the same set of circumstances over and over. In this sense, what transpires in the analysis is at first not experienced as being nearly as familiar as it really is.

But in pointing out what has transpired between them, the analyst can help the patient to recognize a pattern to his personal relations and to see how this pattern relates to the more private states that are also a central concern of analysis. A stance of seeming neutrality excludes much discussion of what happens between the two people in the room, focusing the analysis almost exclusively on the private states themselves rather than on how they are a part of a context of evolving relationship. This has of course been the traditional focus of analysis. But it should not be one's exclusive or preponderant focus if one takes the insights of the interpersonal point of view seriously.

What is at issue is not simply a matter of the analyst's using his own reactions as a clue about what is going on in the patient. Such a use of countertransference feelings as a private guide to empathic understanding is already part of psychoanalytic methodology (Epstein and Feiner 1979). It is certainly useful and important but it is not enough. Usually it accompanies, at least in the classical approach, a focus on the patient alone. There is rarely, in the classical tradition, a confirmation of the patient's experience, even where it is correctly apprehended. So long as the analyst hides behind a "neutral" self-presentation, so long as his own participation in the session's events does not become part of the focus of what he discusses with the patient, it remains difficult for the patient to understand his own experience, and how he goes about creating and re-creating it in his daily life.

A central concern of proponents of the concept of neutrality is that any other stance will interfere with full exploration of the patient's conflicting inclinations. As Schafer (1983) puts it, "the analyst who remains neutral is attempting to allow all of the conflictual material to be fully represented, interpreted, and worked through" (p. 6). To side with any particular view or inclination of the patient can seem to mean standing against another, since conflict is so pervasively a characteristic of psychic life. What the analyst strives to create, says Schafer, is an "atmosphere of safety" in which the analysand feels it is safe to reveal any aspect of himself.

There is an important kernel of truth in this position. It is essential that the analyst continually keep in mind the ubiquity of conflict and be aware of the various subjective meanings that even apparent approval can have to the patient. But several considerations suggest that "neutrality" is not the best way to deal with this issue.

Though Schafer shows greater appreciation than most analysts of the far-reaching implications of Freud's (1926) revised theory of anxiety, he does not go quite far enough. The new centrality of anxiety in clinical theory points to the critical importance of helping the patient most of all to overcome his fears and inhibitions. Given the intensity of infantile fears, which generate neurotic patterns, and of the continuing anxieties that help keep them going, neutrality is simply too weak a stance. I believe that a more positively affirmative stance is required. In this sense, Rogers' term "unconditional positive regard" is a better one than neutrality. But Rogers and his followers tend to exhibit the same confusion that has characterized psychoanalytic discussions on the topic, a confusion between regard for the person and regard for any particular act or idea. It is the former that is crucial for the patient to experience. . . . What the patient needs to learn is that disapproval of something he does is not the same as rejection of him as a person. If the analyst runs scared, if he organizes his whole therapeutic effort around avoiding anything that could smack of disapproval of any thought or act, rather than concerning himself simply with maintaining an overall affirmative attitude toward the patient as a person, he ends up depriving the patient of a crucial learning experience. Being able to acknowledge that, "Yes, my encouragement of your taking an assertive step in the face of your anxieties does mean I prefer your doing that to your opting to hold back, as you sometimes also feel like doing," can be combined with pointing out, "But you experience it as if I would be utterly disgusted with you and totally reject you if you did something I didn't approve of." And, one could add (if one adopted throughout the stance recommended here instead of one of neutrality), "You've seen me not like a particular choice you made in the past. Did it in fact lead to the kind of total rift you fear?" What is crucial, of course, is not the words per se but the repeated experience of being valued as a person regardless of the other's attitude about particular acts.

Even apart from the above, there is reason to question whether refraining from making overt judgments actually facilitates the patient's feeling safer and freer to express a wider range of his thoughts and feelings. There is reason to think that the analyst's stance of ambiguity can at times increase the patient's anxiety, making it more pervasive. Without clear indications of how the analyst is reacting, the anxious patient can sense potential disapproval over everything he says. When the analyst is less covert about his reactions to what the patient says, it can help reassure the patient that when the analyst does not express a negative reaction, he really means it.

When the analyst is consistently ambiguous, the patient's proclivities to experience disapproval are given free reign. This may be useful for the purpose of exploring those proclivities themselves (and occasional technical use of ambiguity and silence—followed at some point by clarification of what one's reaction really was—can be of considerable value). But it is certainly not a reassuring stance for many patients, for whom the atmosphere of safety is diminished by the lack of feedback. The patient then learns a lot about his resistance (and unfortunately can come to view himself as very resistant) but has less opportunity to explore those aspects of himself he has heretofore fearfully avoided, as he continues to experience self-revelation as dangerous.

For some patients, the stance of neutrality can contribute to their tendency to invalidate their own perceptions and even to doubt their own sanity. Parents serve as mediators of reality for the child, helping him to organize his perceptions and to give meaning to events. Perhaps most important of all in this development is learning to read and understand the emotions of other people. For a variety of reasons, parents frequently (often unconsciously) distort this development in their children by being unclear about their own motives and emotions toward their children—saying they are doing something to be helpful when they are really angry, indicating they are not upset about something when they really are, and so forth. Indeed a good portion of our practices can be traced to such experiences (Levenson 1981, 1983).

By hiding behind the stance of "neutrality" the analyst can interfere with the patient's efforts to overcome the effects of such an upbringing. I have found patients ready to explore the associations, early memories, or recent life events that might hold a clue to a disturbed feeling in the session or in the period between sessions, only to flounder until I indicated that perhaps they were reacting to the fact that I had been sleepy or annoyed or inattentive. Such comments brought enormous relief. The patient had dimly sensed my state but had years of experience in "not noticing" such things. They were all too ready to attribute to arcane recesses of their psyches what were primarily reactions to what I had done right in front of them. Incidents like these in fact are opportunities for significant corrective experiences for the patient, but if the analyst's ideology makes such frank revelation of his experience unseemly they can be countertherapeutic instead.

This is not to say that the analyst should simply "let it all hang out." Irresponsibility is hardly an improvement over neutrality. Just as neutrality is a myth at one end of the spectrum, so too is symmetry at the other. Although in one sense patient and therapist are assuredly equals—both are "more simply human than otherwise" and equally deserving of respect and human dignity—the relation is nonetheless asymmetrical. One is asking the other for help. Sometimes the help seeker is the healthier of the two. Often the helper gets a good deal himself from the process. But the asymmetry still stands. The roles and responsibilities of the two parties are different. The patterns of one person's life are the focus of both. Consequently, where one of the two people (the patient) is free to say and reveal whatever he wants, the other (the therapist or analyst) does so only judiciously, when he thinks it will be helpful.

I wish there were very clear rules as to just when such revelations are helpful. Unfortunately there are not, and those with a great need for certainty are likely to prefer a set of premises that give at least the appearance of consistency. This is unfortunate, because the therapist's reactions cannot really be eliminated or hidden. They can only be removed as a topic to address explicitly. In this way, rather than serving as a focus for clarification of the interpersonal patterns the patient gets involved in, they remain vague and unarticulated and become instead a further source of mystification.

This goes for interpretations as well. No less than advice, encouragement, self-disclosure, or technical recommendations, interpretations inevitably convey an attitudinal meta-message as well as the explicit content intended. In addition to illuminating the meaning of some thought or experience of the patient, interpretations, depending on how they are couched, tend to be either invitations or admonitions. The prevailing emphasis on neutrality has led to insufficient attention to the impact of alternative ways of conveying to the patient information about what he is warding off. Consequently interpretations are often unwittingly cast in a manner that is therapeutically counterproductive (Wachtel 1980; see also the discussions by Wile [1982, 1983]).

It is easy for proponents of neutrality to feel that critics are attacking a straw man. It is certainly true that modern defenses of neutrality do not suggest that the analyst really can or should be a blank screen, or advocate the cold, surgeonlike attitude that Freud's metaphors led some incorrectly to assume was appropriate. Writers such as Stone (1961) and Greenson (1967) have presented a far more flexible and humane vision of the analyst's stance. Schafer (1983) notes that "there is always room in analytic work for courtesy, cordiality, gentleness, sincere empathic participation and comment, and other such personal, though not socially intimate, modes of relationship." He later adds a "respectful affirmative attitude" and an attitude of "appreciation."

Thus over the years much that is humane and sensible has accrued to the account of neutrality. Indeed we have reached the point where some analysts now advocate what might best be called a nonneutral neutrality. In the many efforts to clarify that neutrality does not mean cold, distant, uncaring, stiff, impersonal, and so forth, advocates of neutrality are at the same time demonstrating the difficulties with the idea of neutrality itself. For what they are saying is that the usual meanings of neutral are misleading and that they mean neutral in a way that is in many respects quite at odds with how the term can be expected to be taken. But language has consequences. Even the most advanced and sophisticated of analysts, I contend, are constrained by the necessity to show that they are in at least some way "neutral." The dangers such constraint prevents are, in my view, outweighed by the opportunities for creative intervention that are foregone.

It is useful to recognize that at root neutrality is really more a tactic than a basic philosophical position. Consider, for example, Anna Freud's widely cited formulation that the analyst should be equidistant from ego, id, and superego. Close scrutiny of the logic of psychoanalytic theory suggests a different perspective on this recommendation than is usually offered. Consider the following discussion drawn from an extended examination of the social implications of Sigmund Freud's ideas:

Freud's effort to make the unconscious conscious had . . . the quality of a search and destroy mission. . . . Freud was essentially a sophisticated conservative who knew that, like a village that flies the flag but harbors guerrillas, the civilized psyche could not be secure, and certainly could not prosper, until the enemy was brought to light. Once out of hiding, it could be better controlled or perhaps reformed. "Where id was, let ego be" is clearly not a formula for expanding the territory of the id. It points rather to a repatriation program.

The ego . . . is ultimately Freud's real ally in the psyche. . . . The common recommendation to analysts that they maintain an even-handed neutrality among ego, id, and superego must be understood as a tactical rather than a strategic recommendation. Only by enabling the id and the superego to reveal themselves, by not taking a stance that will drive them underground, can the conditions be established whereby the ego can be strengthened. But make no mistake: It is the ego that must come out the winner. [Wachtel 1983, p. 216].

A neutral-seeming stance then can be useful for tactical purposes. But neutrality is a concept both too watery and too negative to provide the main guide to therapeutic work.

I have not been concerned with drawing a sharp distinction between psychoanalysis and psychotherapy. This is not through oversight but a very conscious intention. It is my belief that all too often the question, "Is it analysis?" takes precedence over, "Is it good for the patient?" Psychoanalysis is, after all, but a form of psychotherapy. Freud himself believed that psychoanalysis as a theory of the mind would stand long after the specific therapeutic technique called psychoanalysis had become obsolete. Excessive concern with distinguishing psychoanalysis from all other psychotherapies—even among interpersonalists—has exerted a powerful conservative constraint on the development of a more effective psychotherapy, informed by psychoanalytic insights but free to evolve in ways that go beyond our present ability to be helpful.

REFERENCES

Epstein. L., and Feiner, A. H. (1979). *The Therapist's Contribution to the Therapeutic Situation*. New York: Jason Aronson.

Freud, S. (1926). Inhibitions, symptoms, and anxiety. *Standard Edition* 21:87–172.

Gill, M. (1979). The analysis of transference. *Journal of the American Psychoanalytic Association* 27: (Suppl.) 263–288.

Greenson, R. (1967). *The Technique and Practice of Psychoanalysis*. New York: International Universities Press.

Levenson, E. (1981). Facts and fantasies: the nature of analytic data. *Contemporary Psychoanalysis* 17:486–500.

_____ (1983). *The Ambiguity of Change*. New York: Basic Books.

Schafer, R. (1983). *The Analytic Attitude*. New York: Basic Books.

Stone, L. (1961). *The Psychoanalytic Situation*. New York: International Universities Press.

Wachtel, P. L. (1977a). *Psychoanalysis and Behavior Therapy*. New York: Basic Books.

_____ (1977b). Interaction cycles, unconscious processes, and the person-situation issue. In *Personality at the Crossroads: Issues in Interactional Psychology*, ed. D. Magnusson and N. Endler, pp. 317–331. Hillsdale, NJ: Lawrence Erlbaum.

_____ (1980). What should we say to our patients: on the wording of therapists' comments to patients. *Psychotherapy: Theory, Research and Practice* 17:183–188.

_____ (1981). Transference, schema and assimilation: the relevance of Piaget to the psychoanalytic theory of transference. In *The Annual of Psychoanalysis*, vol. 8, pp. 69–76. New York: International Universities Press.

_____ (1982). Vicious circles: the self and the rhetoric of emerging and unfolding. *Contemporary Psychoanalysis* 18:273–295.

_____ (1983). *The Poverty of Affluence*. New York: The Free Press.

Wile, D. (1982). *Couples Therapy*. New York: Wiley.

_____ (1983). Kohut, Kernberg, and accusatory interpretations. Paper delivered at the Annual Meeting of the American Psychological Association.

Wolf, E. (1966). Learning theory and psychoanalysis. *British Journal of Medical Psychology* 39:1–10.

5

The Patient as Interpreter of the Analyst's Experience[1]

Irwin Z. Hoffman

EDITOR'S SYNOPSIS

In this paper Hoffman explains how transference analysis may be furthered through exploration of the patient's ideas as to the therapist's experience in therapy. Insight into transference is facilitated by seeking out what the patient has tried to evoke, as well as what he has actually evoked in the therapist. To do so the therapist relies on both his own and the patient's ideas regarding therapist reactions to the patient.

Hoffman begins with the concept of the blank screen. Conservatively taken, this concept represents the viewpoint that the patient's experience in therapy is significantly detached from the actual presence of the therapist. A counterpart to this is a definition of transference as representing the patient's distortion of current reality, a distortion to be noted and interpreted by the

[1]This paper was published in *Contemporary Psychoanalysis*, 1983; 19(3): 389–422.

therapist. These notions are rejected by Hoffman. The patient's transference reaction is viewed as having a basis in the here-and-now interaction. Transference is seen as having three distinguishing features: the patient's selective attention to certain behaviors in others, a predisposition to choose one set of interpretations regarding behavior over possible others, and a tendency to behave in a manner that elicits responses consistent with one's expectations. Transference is viewed as a means of construing and constructing relationships. The patient selectively attends to things that conform to expectations and also behaves in a fashion that elicits reactions confirming what is already held to be true.

To understand a patient's transference one must give credence to the patient's view of the relationship, particularly his interpretation of the therapist's reaction to him. The patient is viewed as having a plausible, often insightful view of what is occurring between patient and therapist. This viewpoint is to be taken seriously. What is to be avoided is the scenario in which the therapist's opinions are deemed correct and the patient's a distortion of reality.

Hoffman observes that patients create atmospheres in therapy. This atmosphere includes the therapist's reaction to the patient and the patient's reaction to the therapist based on what he thinks he has elicited in the therapist. It is felt that at some level the patient is aware of his impact on the therapist, that he unconsciously senses his transference prodding will elicit certain responses in the therapist. The patient is, however, unsure of the extent this impact will induce the therapist into joining the patient in enactment of conflicted neurotic patterns. The therapist has the task of disapproving the patient's expectation by disengaging from the patient's transference-based maneuvers, at the same time offering the patient the possibility of a new experience in relating.

Through his emphasis on the patient as a potentially accurate and astute participant in the understanding of the therapeutic interaction, Hoffman contributes to effective work with transference. His ideas help transform transference analysis from a situation where one person acts upon another by means of interpretation, to a collaborative, two-person examination of the relationship.

INTRODUCTION

This paper presents a point of view on the psychoanalytic situation and on psychoanalytic technique through, in part, a selective review of the literature. An important underlying assumption of the paper is that existing theoretical models inevitably influence and reflect practice. This is often true even of models that practitioners claim they do not take seriously or literally. Such models may continue to affect practice adversely as long as their features are not fully appreciated and as long as alternative models are not recognized or integrated. An example of such a lingering model is the one in which the therapist is said to function like a blank screen in the psychoanalytic situation.

THE RESILIENCE OF THE BLANK SCREEN CONCEPT

The psychoanalytic literature is replete with attacks on the blank screen concept, the idea that the analyst is not accurately perceived by the patient as a real person, but that he serves rather as a screen or mirror to whom various attitudes, feelings, and motives can be attributed depending upon the patient's particular neurosis and its transference expression. Critiques of this idea have come from within the ranks of classical Freudian analysts, as well as from Kleinians and Sullivanians. Even if one looks only at the classical literature, in one way or another, the blank screen concept seems to have been pronounced dead and laid to rest many times over the years. In 1950, Ida Macalpine, addressing only the implications for the patient's experience of classical psychoanalytic technique as she conceived of it (that is, not considering the analyst's personal contributions), said the following:

It can *no longer be maintained* that the analysand's reactions in analysis occur spontaneously. His behavior is a response to the rigid infantile setting to which he is exposed. This poses many problems for further investigation. One of them is how does it react upon the patient? He must know it, consciously or unconsciously. [p. 526, italics added]

Theresa Benedek said in 1953:

As the history of psychoanalysis shows, the discussion of countertransference usually ended in a retreat to defensive positions. The argument to this end *used to be* [italics added] that the classical attitude affords the best guarantee that the *personality of the therapist* [author's italics] would not enter the action-field of the therapeutic process. By that one assumes that as long as the analyst does not reveal himself as a person, does not answer questions regarding his own personality, he remains unknown as if without individuality, that the transference process may unfold and be motivated only by the patient's resistances. The patient—although he is a sensitive, neurotic individual—is not supposed to sense and discern the therapist as a person. [p. 202]

In 1956 Lucia Tower wrote:

I have for a very long time speculated that in many—perhaps every—intensive analytic treatment there develops something in the nature of countertransference structures (perhaps even a "neurosis") which are essential and inevitable counterparts of the transference neurosis. [p. 232]

In the 1960s Loewald (1960), Stone (1961), and Greenson (1965) added their voices to the already large chorus of protest against this remarkably resilient concept. From varying theoretical perspectives, the critiques continued into the 1970s and 1980s as represented, for example, in the writings of Gill (1979, 1982a, 1982b, 1983, Gill and Hoffman 1982a, 1982b), Sandler (1976, 1981) and Kohut (1977), among many others. In fact, the blank screen idea is probably not articulated as often or even as well by its proponents as it is by its opponents, a situation that leads inevitably to the suspicion that the proponents are straw men and that shooting them down has become a kind of popular psychoanalytic sport.[2]

I am persuaded, however, that the issue is a very important one and that it deserves repeated examination and discussion. The blank screen view in psychoanalysis is only one instance of a much broader phenomenon that might be termed *asocial conceptions of the patient's experience in psychotherapy*. According to these conceptions, there is a stream of experience going on in the patient that is divorced to a significant extent from the immediate impact of the therapist's personal presence. I say "personal presence" because generally certain theoretically prescribed facilitating aspects of the therapist's conduct are recognized fully as affecting the course of the patient's experience. But the paradigm is one in which proper or ideal conduct on the part of the therapist allows for a flow of experience that has an organic-like momentum of its own and that is free to follow a certain "natural" course. An intriguing example of this asocial paradigm outside of psychoanalysis can be found in client-centered therapy. Ideally, the classical client-centered therapist is so totally and literally self-effacing that his personality as such is effectively removed from the patient's purview. Carl Rogers stated in 1951:

It is surprising how frequently the client uses the word "impersonal" in describing the therapeutic relationship after the conclusion of therapy. This is obviously not intended to mean that the relationship was cold or disinterested. It appears to be the client's attempt to describe this unique experience in which the person of the counselor—the counselor as an

---

[2]It is interesting that critics of the blank screen concept have frequently been concerned that others would think they were beating a dead horse (see, for example, Sterba 1934, p. 117, Stone 1961, pp. 18–19, and Kohut 1977, pp. 253–255).

evaluating, reacting person with needs of his own—is so clearly absent. In this sense it is "im"-personal . . . the whole relationship is composed of the self of the client, the counselor being de-personalized for the purposes of therapy into being "the client's other self." [p. 208]

In psychoanalysis, the blank screen idea persists in more or less qualified and more or less openly acknowledged forms.[3] The counterpart of the notion that the analyst functions like a screen is the definition of transference as a distortion of current reality. As Szasz (1963) has pointed out, this definition of transference can serve a very important defensive function for the analyst. This function may partly account for the persistence of the concept. I believe that another factor that has kept it alive has been the confusion of two issues. One has to do with the optimal level of spontaneity and personal involvement that the analyst should express in the analytic situation. The other has to do with the kind of credibility that is attributed to the patient's ideas about the analyst's experience. A theorist may repudiate the notion that the analyst should behave in an aloof, impersonal manner without addressing the question of the tenability of the patient's transference-based speculations about the analyst's experience. To anticipate what follows, such speculations may touch upon aspects of the analyst's response to the patient, which the analyst thinks is well-concealed or of which he himself is unaware. In general, recommendations pertaining to the analyst's personal conduct in the analytic situation may very well leave intact the basic model according to which the transference is understood and interpreted.

STANDARD QUALIFICATIONS OF THE
BLANK SCREEN CONCEPT

The notion that ideally the analyst functions like a screen is always qualified in the sense that it applies to only a part of the

---

[3]Dewald's (1972) depiction of his conduct of an analysis exemplifies, as Lipton (1982) has shown, a relatively pure, if implicit, blank screen position.

patient's total experience of the therapist, the part that is conventionally regarded as neurotic transference. This is the aspect of the patient's experience that, allegedly, distorts reality because of the persisting influence of childhood events, wishes, conflicts, and adaptations. There are two kinds of experience that even the staunchest proponents of the screen or mirror function of the analyst recognize as likely to be responsive to something in the analyst's actual behavior rather than as expressions of pure fantasy. One is the patient's perception of the analyst as essentially trustworthy and competent, a part of the patient's experience that Freud (1912) subsumed under the rubric of the unobjectionable positive transference but that others, most notably Sterba (1934), Greenson (1965), and Zetzel (1956) have chosen to exclude from the realm of transference, designating it as the experience of the working or therapeutic alliance.[4] The second is the patient's recognition of and response to relatively blatant expressions of the therapist's neurotic and antitherapeutic countertransference. Both categories of experience lie outside the realm of transference proper, which is where we find the patient's unfounded ideas, his neurotic, intrapsychically determined fantasies about the therapist. The point is well represented in the following statements (quoted here in reverse order) that are part of a classical definition of transference (Moore and Fine 1968):

[1] Transference should be carefully differentiated from the therapeutic alliance, a conscious aspect of the relationship between analyst and patient. In this, each implicitly agrees and understands their working together to help the analysand to mature through *insight*, progressive understanding, and control.

[2] One of the important reasons for the relative anonymity of the analyst during the treatment process is the fact that a lack of information about his real attributes in personal life facilitates a transfer of the patient's revived early images on to his person. It also lessens the distortion of fantasies from the past by present perceptions. It must be

---

[4]For discussions of the implications of Freud's position on this matter see Lipton (1977a) and Gill (1982a, pp. 9–15).

recognized that there are situations or circumstances where the actual behavior or attitudes of the analyst cause reactions in the patient; these are not considered part of the transference reaction. [p. 93]

TWO TYPES OF PARADIGMS AND CRITIQUES

In my view, critiques of the screen concept can be classified into two major categories: conservative critiques and radical critiques. Conservative critiques, in effect, always take the following form: they argue that one or both of the standard qualifications of the blank screen view noted above have been underemphasized or insufficiently elaborated in terms of their role in the analytic process. I call these critiques conservative because they retain the notion that a crucial aspect of the patient's experience of the therapist has little or no relation to the therapist's actual behavior or actual attitudes. The conservative critic reserves the term *transference* for this aspect of the patient's experience. At the same time he objects to a failure to recognize sufficiently the importance of another aspect of the patient's experience that is influenced by the "real" characteristics of the therapist, whether these real characteristics promote or interfere with an ideal analytic process. The dichotomy between realistic and unrealistic perception may be considered less sharp, but it is nevertheless retained. Although the realistic aspects of the patient's experience are now given more careful consideration and weight, in relation to transference proper the therapist is no less a blank screen than he was before. By not altering the standard paradigm for defining what is or is not realistic in the analytic situation, conservative critiques of the blank screen fallacy always end up perpetuating that very fallacy.

In contrast to conservative critiques, radical critiques reject the dichotomy between transference as distortion and nontransference as reality based. They argue instead that transference itself always has a significant plausible basis in the here and now. The radical critic of the blank screen model denies that there is any aspect of the patient's experience that pertains to the therapist's inner motives that can be unequivocally designated as distorting of reality. Similarly, he denies that there is any aspect of this experience that can be unequivocally designated as faithful to reality. The radical critic is a relativist. From his point of view the perspective that the patient brings to bear in interpreting the therapist's inner attitudes is regarded as one among many perspectives that are relevant, each of which highlights different facets of the analyst's involvement. This amounts to a different paradigm, not simply an elaboration of the standard paradigm which is what the conservative critics propose.

In rejecting the proposition that transference-dominated experience and nontransference-dominated experience can be differentiated on the grounds that the former is represented by fantasy that is divorced from reality whereas the latter is reality based, the radical critic does not imply that the two types of experience cannot be distinguished. Indeed, having rejected the criterion of distorted versus realistic perception, he is obliged to offer other criteria according to which this distinction can be made. For the radical critic the distinguishing features of the neurotic transference have to do with the fact that the patient is selectively attentive to certain facets of the therapist's behavior and personality; that he is compelled to choose one set of interpretations rather than others; that his emotional life and adaptation are unconsciously governed by and governing of the particular viewpoint he has adopted; and, perhaps most importantly, that he has behaved in such a way as to actually elicit overt and covert responses that are consistent with his viewpoint and expectations. The transference represents a way not only of construing but also of constructing or shaping interpersonal relations in general and the relationship with the analyst in particular. One could retain the term *distortion* only if it is defined in terms of the sense of necessity that the patient attaches to what he makes happen and to what he sees as happening between himself and the analyst.

The radical critiques are opposed not merely to the blank screen idea but to any model that suggests that the "objective" or "real" impact of the therapist is equivalent to what he intends or to what he thinks his overt behavior has conveyed or betrayed. What the radical critic refuses to do is to consign the patient's ideas about the analyst's hidden motives and attitudes to the realm of unfounded fantasy whenever those ideas depart from the analyst's judgment of his own intentions. In this respect, whether the analyst's manifest conduct is cold or warm or even self-disclosing is not the issue. What matters to the radical critic in determining whether a particular model is based on an asocial or truly social conception of the patient's experience is whether the patient is considered capable of understanding, if only preconsciously, that there is more to the therapist's experience than what meets the eye, even more than what meets the mind's eye of the therapist at any given moment. More than challenging the blank screen fallacy, the radical critic challenges what might be termed *the naive patient fallacy*, the notion that the patient, insofar as he is rational, takes the analyst's behavior at face value even while his own is continually scrutinized for the most subtle indications of unspoken or unconscious meanings.

IMPLICATIONS OF THE AMBIGUITY OF THE
ANALYST'S CONDUCT IN THE ANALYTIC SITUATION

There is an underlying view of reality that the radical critiques of the screen concept share. This view is simply that reality is not a preestablished given or absolute. As Wachtel (1980) says, arguing from the perspective of Piaget's theory of cognitive development: "neither as children or as adults do we respond directly to stimuli per se. We are always constructing reality every bit as much as we are perceiving it" (p. 62). Moreover, the realm of interpersonal events is distinguished from that of physical events in that "such events are highly ambiguous, and consensus is much harder to obtain" (p. 69).

Keep in mind that we have as our principal concern one person's ideas (which may or may not be conscious themselves) about another person's experience. The other person's experience can only be inferred; it is never directly visible as such. Although we may believe we recognize signs of it in verbal and nonverbal behavior, the relationship between such signs and actual experience is always uncertain. When we think about patients, we know that there may well be discrepancies between what a patient says and what he consciously thinks as well as discrepancies between what he consciously thinks and what he vaguely senses but resists facing up to in himself. We know that the relation between what is manifest and what is latent may be extraordinarily complex. We know this of our patients and in a general way of ourselves. What we are prone to ignore or deny, however, is that this ambiguity and complexity applies to the way in which the therapist participates in the therapeutic process. As Racker (1968) says:

The first distortion of truth in "the myth of the analytic situation" is that analysis is an interaction between a sick person and a healthy one. The truth is that it is an interaction between two personalities, in both of which the ego is under pressure from the id, the superego, and the external world; each personality has its internal and external dependencies, anxieties, and pathological defenses; each is also a child with his internal parents; and each of these whole personalities—that of the analysand and that of the analyst—responds to every event in the analytic situation. [p. 132]

And in another chapter Racker (1968) says, "The analyst's relation to his patient is a libidinal one and is a constant emotional experience" (p. 31).

The safeguards of the analytic situation do not prevent the analyst from having this "constant emotional experience." What is more, every patient senses this, consciously or preconsciously. Also every patient brings to bear his own particular perspective in interpreting the meaning of the analyst's manifest behavior as it communicates, conveys, or inadvertently betrays something in the analyst's personal experience. The fact that a particular perspective may be charged with tremendous significance and importance for the patient does not nullify its plausibility. If anything the opposite may be the case. The patient's transference predisposition acts as a kind of Geiger counter that picks up aspects of the analyst's personal response in the analytic situation that might otherwise remain hidden. As Benedek (1953) put it:

Rarely does one realize that the patient, under the pressure of his emotional needs—needs which may be motivated by the frustration of transference—may grope for the therapist as a real person, may sense his reactions and will sometimes almost read his mind . . . Yes, the patient . . . bores his way into the preconscious mind of the therapist and often emerges with surprising evidences of empathy—of preconscious awareness of the therapist's personality and even of his problems. [p. 203]

What the patient's transference accounts for is not a distortion of reality but a selective attention to and sensitivity to certain facets of the analyst's highly ambiguous response to the patient in the analysis. What one patient notices about the analyst another ignores. What matters to one may not matter to another, or may matter in a different way. One could make a case for using the term *distortion* for just this kind of selective attention and sensitivity, but that is not usually the way the term is used and I do think it would be misleading. After all, it is not as though one could describe the "real analyst" or the true nature of the analyst's experience independent of any selective attention and sensitivity. As Wachtel (1980) says:

To be sure, each patient's experience of the analyst is highly individual and shaped by personal needs and fantasies. But consider the enormous variation in perception of the analyst by those other than his patients— the differences in how he is experienced by his spouse, his children, his teachers, his students, his friends, his rivals. Which is the "undistorted" standard from which the transference distortion varies? [pp. 66-67][5]

---

[5]In what seems to me to be a non sequitur, Wachtel retreats from the implications of this position at the end of his paper (p. 74) and accepts the term *distortion* in a manner that contradicts the heart of his argument.

There is no perception free of some kind of preexisting set or bias or expectation, or, to borrow from Piaget's framework, no perception independent of "assimilation" to some preexisting schema. Such assimilation does not twist an absolute external reality into something it is not. Rather it gives meaning or shape to something "out there" that has among its "objective" properties a kind of amenability to being assimilated in just this way. Moreover, the schema itself is flexible and tends to accommodate to what is in the environment even while it makes what is in the environment fit itself. Thus, turning to the clinical situation that concerns us, a patient who, for example, has a readiness to feel used, may detect and be selectively attentive and sensitive to whatever qualifies as a plausible indication of an exploitative motive on the part of the particular analyst he is seeing. With one analyst it might be his high fee, with another his use of a tape recorder for research purposes, with another his use of the therapy for his own training, with another his (allegedly) sadistic use of silence, with another his (allegedly) sadistic use of active interpretation.

The analytic situation is comprised of only two people—both of whom are participating in a charged interpersonal interaction that can result in either one of them resisting recognizing something in himself that the other discerns. From the perspective of the radical critic, it behooves the analyst to operate with this skepticism about what he knows of himself at a particular moment always in mind and to regard the patient as a potentially astute interpreter of his (the analyst's) own resisted internal motives. In fact, in some cases a patient with a particular "transference predisposition" (a phrase that Racker uses that is comparable to the notion of schema) may guess something about the countertransference that most other independent judges would not have picked up. As Gill and I have written (1982b):

In some instances, a group of judges may agree that the therapist has behaved in a particular way, one which could be construed as seductive, or disapproving or whatever, only after some subtle aspect of his behavior is called to their attention by another single observer. This observer, might of course, be none other than the patient. [p. 140]

Not despite the influence of the transference but because of it:

[The patient] may notice something about the therapist's behavior or suggest a possible interpretation of it that most judges would overlook. Nevertheless, once it is called to their attention, they may all agree that the patient's perceptions and inferences were quite plausible. [p. 140]

IMPLICATIONS OF THE RESPONSIVENESS OF THE ANALYST'S EXPERIENCE IN THE PSYCHOANALYTIC SITUATION

In what I have said so far I have deliberately contrived to deemphasize the second major consideration that addresses the implication of the analyst's personal presence for the transference. I have done this in order to take the argument associated with the ambiguous nature of the analyst's involvement as far as I could. But it is the second consideration, coupled with the first, that I think clinches the argument of the radical critic that the patient's plausible interpretations of the analyst's experience be considered part of the transference and that the transference not be defined in terms of perceptual distortion.

This second consideration is simply that the analyst in the analytic situation is continually having some sort of personal affective reaction that is a response to the patient's manner of relating to him. What is more, every patient knows that he is influencing the analyst's experience and that the freedom the analyst has to resist this influence is limited. Patients create atmospheres in analysis—atmospheres that we sometimes actually speak of as though something were "in the air" between the participants. These atmospheres include the therapist's personal reaction to the patient, the patient guessing what the reaction is partly on the basis of what he thinks his own behavior is likely to have elicited, the analyst guessing what the patient is guessing, and so on.

Sandler (1976) puts it this way:

In the transference, in many subtle ways, the patient attempts to prod the analyst into behaving in a particular way and unconsciously scans and adapts to his perceptions of the analyst's reaction. The analyst may be able to "hold" his response to this "prodding" in his consciousness as a reaction *of his own* which he perceives, and I would make the link between certain countertransference responses and transference via the behavioral (verbal and non-verbal) *interaction* between the patient and the analyst. [p. 44]

Sandler's emphasis on the analyst's behavior as a basis upon which the patient concludes (preconsciously) that he has elicited the response he is looking for underestimates the extent to which the patient's ideas about the countertransference can flow directly and plausibly from what he knows about the evocative nature of his own behavior. However the analyst believes he has behaved, if the patient thinks he has been continually deprecating, or harshly critical, he has reason to believe that the analyst may feel somewhat hurt, or that he may experience a measure of irritation and a wish to retaliate. Such ideas do not require perceptual confirmation in order for the patient to believe, with reason, that they are plausible. The perceptual confirmation might follow in any number of ways. For example, if the analyst keeps his cool and shows not the slightest bit of irritation, the patient might well imagine that this is precisely the expression of the analyst's revenge, that is, that the analyst will not give the patient the satisfaction of thinking he can affect him in a personal way. And, undoubtedly, ostensible adherence to the more austere canons of "proper" analytic conduct can sometimes function as a disguised vehicle for the expression of intense countertransference attitudes on the part of the analyst. However, the perceptual confirmation may be secondary, since from the patient's point of view the die is cast and the outcome is highly likely given his own evocative behavior.

For a theorist like Racker the countertransference is inevitable and his discussion of it carries none of the opprobrium that comes across so heavily and oppressively in the work of Langs. Racker and Heimann take the same step forward with respect to countertransference that Freud took when he moved from thinking of the transference as an obstacle to thinking of transference as the principal vehicle of the analytic process. The countertransference in the social paradigm of the radical critics is likely to embody something resembling aspects of the patient's internal objects or aspects of the patient's self-representation. Heimann (1950) goes so far as to say, "The analyst's countertransference is not only part and parcel of the analytic relationship, but it is the patient's *creation*, it is part of the patient's personality" (p. 83).

The element of hyperbole in Heimann's position illustrates an error that often appears in discussions of the mechanism of projective identification. Instead of being a blank screen, the analyst becomes an empty "container" (Bion 1962) into which the patient deposits various parts of himself. Although the emphasis is on interaction, the metaphor of the container lends itself, ironically, to yet another asocial conception of the situation since somehow the analyst's personality has once again been extricated from the process (cf. Levenson 1981, p. 492). Nevertheless, the concept of projective identification, with the hyperbolic metaphor removed, does help bridge the alleged gap between the intrapsychic and the interpersonal (Ogden 1979). It should be evident that in this paper the terms *social* and *interpersonal* do not connote something superficial or readily observable from "outside" or something nonintrapsychic, the pejorative connotations that these terms have unfortunately acquired for many classical analysts. Experience that is conceptualized in the terms of the social paradigm is experience that is layered by reciprocal conscious, preconscious, and unconscious responses in each of the participants.[6] What is more, something can "unfold" in the course of the analysis that bears the stamp of the patient's transference predispositions. What is intrapsychic is realized in the patient's idea of the interaction of the transference and the countertransference, which is likely to include a rough approximation of the

---

[6]See Fourcher (1975) for a discussion of human experience as the expression of social reciprocity on multiple levels of psychological organization and consciousness.

quality if not the quantity of the actual countertransference. It is in this element of correspondence between the patient's idea of the countertransference and the actual countertransference that the elusive interface of the intrapsychic and the interpersonal lies.

IMPLICATIONS OF THE SOCIAL PARADIGM FOR TECHNIQUE

The Impact of the Countertransference on the Fate of the Relationship

Because the analyst is human, he is likely to have in his repertoire a blueprint for approximately the emotional response that the patient's transference dictates and that response is likely to be elicited, whether consciously or unconsciously (Searles 1978–1979, pp. 172–173). Ideally this response serves as a key—perhaps the best key the analyst has—to the nature of the interpersonal scene that the patient is driven by transference to create. The patient as interpreter of the analyst's experience suspects that he has created something, the complement of the transference, in the analyst; that is, he suspects it at some level. What he does not know and what remains to be decided, is what role the counter-transference experience of the analyst will have in determining the total nature of the analyst's response to the patient. In other words he does not know the extent to which the countertransference will combine with the transference to determine the destiny of the relationship. The extent to which the analyst's objectivity, the tendency that is inclined toward understanding more than enacting, will prevail and successfully resist the pull of the transference and the countertransference is unknown at any given moment not only to the patient but also to the analyst.

Within the transference itself, there is a kind of self-fulfilling prophecy, and with it, a kind of fatalism, a sense that the outcome is inevitable. The transference includes not just a sense of what has happened or is happening but also a prediction, a conviction even, about what will happen. The attempt to disprove this prediction is an active, ongoing, mutual effort, which is always accompanied by a real element of uncertainty. The analyst's uncertainty has as much if not more to do with his inability to know, in advance, how much his own countertransference will govern his response to his patient as it has to do with his inability to measure, precisely, the patient's resistance and motivation for change. Moreover, the patient, as interpreter of the therapist's experience, has good reason to think and fear that the counter-transference-evoking power of his transferences may be the decisive factor in determining the course of the relationship. Or, to say the same thing in another way, he has good reason to fear that the analyst's constant susceptibility to countertransference will doom the relationship to repeat, covertly if not overtly, the very patterns of interpersonal interaction that he came to analysis to change.

Pitted against the powerful alignment of transference and countertransference is the interest that the patient and the analyst share in making something happen that will be new for the patient and that will promote his ability to develop new kinds of interpersonal relationships. This is where the objectivity of the analyst enters and plays such an important role. It is not an objectivity that enables the analyst to demonstrate to the patient how his transference ideas and expectations distort reality. Instead it is an objectivity that enables the analyst to work to create another kind of interpersonal experience that diverges from the one toward which the transference–countertransference interaction pulls. In this other experience, the patient comes to know that the analyst is not so consumed or threatened by the countertransference that he is no longer able to interpret the transference. For to be able to interpret the transference fully means interpreting, and in some measure being receptive to, the patient's interpretations of the countertransference (Racker 1968, p. 131). What ensues is a subtle kind of rectification. The patient is, in some measure, freed of an unconscious sense of obligation to resist interpreting the analyst's experience in order to accommodate a reciprocal resistance in the analyst. Ironically, the resistance in the patient sometimes takes the form of an apparently fervent belief that, objectively speaking, the analyst must be the very neutral screen that, according to the standard model he aspires to be (see Racker 1968, p. 67). The patient takes the position, in effect, that his ideas about the analyst are nothing but fantasy, derived entirely from his childhood experiences, nothing but transference in the standard sense of the term. In such a case, the analyst must interpret this denial; he must combat this resistance, not collude with it. To the extent that the analyst is objective, to the extent that he keeps himself from "drowning in the countertransference" (Racker 1968, p. 132), which, of course, could take the form of repressing it, to that very extent is he able to actively elicit the patient's preconscious and resisted interpretations of the countertransference and take them in stride.

Interpretation as Rectification

Whether the therapist's response will be dominated by countertransference or not is a question that is raised again and again throughout the course of the therapy, probably in each hour with varying degrees of urgency. Also, it is a question that in many instances cannot begin to be resolved in a favorable direction unless or until a timely interpretation is offered by the therapist. At the very moment that he interprets, the analyst often extricates himself as much as he extricates the patient from transference–countertransference enactment. When the therapist who is experiencing the quality, if not the quantity, of the countertransference reaction that the patient is attributing to him says to the patient, "I think you think I am feeling vulnerable," or "I think you have the impression that I am hiding or denying my hostility toward you" or "my attraction to you," at that moment, at least, he manages to cast doubt on the transference-based expectation that the countertransference will be consuming and will result in defensive adaptations in the analyst complementary to those in the transference. The interpretation is "mutative" (Strachey 1934) partly because it has a certain reflexive impact on the analyst himself that the patient senses. Because it is implicitly self-interpretive it modifies something in the analyst's own experience of the patient. By making it apparent that the countertransference experience that the patient has attributed to the analyst occupies only a part of his response to the patient, the analyst also makes it apparent that he is finding something more in the patient to respond to than the transference-driven provocateur. Not to be minimized as a significant part of this "something more" that the analyst now is implicitly showing a kind of appreciation for is the patient's capacity to understand, empathize with, and interpret the analyst's experience, especially his experience of the patient (cf. Searles 1975).

As Gill (1979) has pointed out, the patient, through the analysis of the transference, has a new interpersonal experience that is inseparable from the collaborative development of insight into the transference itself. This new experience is most powerful when the insight into the transference includes a new understanding of what the patient has tried to evoke and what he has plausibly construed as having been actually evoked in the analyst. The rectification that I spoke of earlier of the patient's unconscious need to accommodate to a resistance that is attributed to the analyst is also more likely when the analyst is able to find the patient's interpretation of the countertransference in associations that are not manifestly about the psychoanalytic situation at all. When he does this, he demonstrates to the patient that rather than being defensive about the patient's ideas about the countertransference, he actually has an appetite for them and is eager to seek them out.

Systematic use of the patient's associations as a guide to understanding the patient's resisted ideas about the countertransference is a critical element of the interpretive process in the social paradigm. Without it, there is a danger that the analyst will rely excessively on his own subjective experience in constructing interpretations. The analyst then risks making the error of automatically assuming that what he feels corresponds with what the patient attributes to him. In fact, Racker (1968), whom I have cited so liberally, seems to invite this criticism at times, although he also warns against regarding the experience of the countertransference as oracular (p. 170). It is true that in many cases the most powerful interpretations are constructed out of a convergence of something in the analyst's personal response and a theme in the patient's associations. However, there are other instances when the associations suggest a latent interpretation of the analyst's experience that comes as a surprise to the analyst and overrides what he might have guessed based upon his awareness of his internal state. Thus, continually reading the patient's associations for their allusions to the countertransference via the mechanisms of displacement and identification (Gill 1979, 1982a; Gill and Hoffman 1982a, 1982b; Lipton 1977b) is a necessary complement to the analyst's countertransference experience in constructing interpretations and ensures that the patient's perspective, as reflected in the content of his communications, is not overshadowed by what the analyst is aware of in himself.

The Role of Enactment and Confession of Countertransference

The new experience that the patient has is something that the participants make happen and that they are frequently either on the verge of failing to make happen or actually failing to make happen. That is, they are frequently either on the verge of enacting transference–countertransference patterns or actually in the midst of enacting them, even if in muted or disguised ways. Where Gill, Racker, Searles, and Levenson, among others, differ from conservative critics like Langs is in their acceptance of a certain thread of transference–contertransference enactment throughout the analysis that stands in a kind of dialectic relationship with the process by which this enactment, as experienced by the patient, is analyzed.

I want to be clear that nothing I have said requires admission on the part of the analyst of actual countertransference experiences. On the contrary, I think the extra factor of objectivity that the analyst has to help combat the pull of the transference and the countertransference usually rests precisely on the fact that the nature of his participation in the interaction is different from that of the patient. This is what increases the likelihood that he will be able to subordinate his countertransference reactions to the purposes of the analysis. What Racker (1968) speaks of as "the myth of the analytic situation," namely, that it is an interaction "between a sick person and a healthy one" (p. 132), is, ironically, perpetuated by those who argue that regular countertransference confessions should be incorporated as part of psychoanalytic technique.[7] Such regular self-disclosure is likely to pull the therapist's total personality into the exchange in the same manner that it would be involved in other intimate social relationships. To think that the analyst will have any special capability in such circumstances to resist neurotic forms of reciprocal reenactment would have to be based on an assumption that his mental health is vastly superior to that of the patient. Admissions of counter-transference responses also tend to imply an overestimation of the therapist's conscious experience at the expense of what is resisted and is preconscious or unconscious. Similarly it implies an extraordinary ability on the part of the analyst to capture the essence of his experience of the patient in a few words whereas the patient may grope for hours in his free association before he reaches a verbalization that fully captures something in his experience of the analyst. Another way of saying this is that countertransference confessions encourage an illusion that the participants may share that the element of ambiguity that is associated with the analyst's conduct and that leaves it open to a variety of plausible interpretations has now been virtually elimi-nated. Once the analyst says what he feels there is likely to be an increment of investment on his part in being taken at his word. This is an increment of investment that the patient will sense and try to accommodate so that the reciprocal resistance to the

---

[7]Bollas (1983) has recently discussed and illustrated the usefulness of *occasional* judicious disclosures by the analyst of his countertransfer-ence predicament.

patient's continuing interpretation of the therapist's inner experience can become very powerful.

Although countertransference confessions are usually ill-advised, there are times when a degree of personal, self-revealing expressiveness is not only inescapable but desirable (Bollas 1983, Ehrenberg 1982). In fact, there are times when the only choices available to the analyst are a variety of emotionally expressive responses. Neither attentive listening nor interpretation of any kind is necessarily a way out of this predicament because the patient may have created an atmosphere in which customary analytic distance is likely to be experienced by both participants as inordinately withholding, compulsive, or phony. As long as the ambiance is such that the patient and the analyst both know that whatever is going on more than likely has meaning that is not yet being spoken of or explored but eventually will be, openly expressive interpersonal interactions may do more good than harm and may continue for some time before it becomes possible to interpret them retrospectively in a spirit that holds any hope of benefit for the patient. In other words, it may be some time before the act of interpreting will become sufficiently free of destructive countertransference meaning so that the patient can hear and make use of the content of the intervention.

Again, it is not that instead of interpreting in such circumstances one should merely wait silently, but rather that a certain specific kind of spontaneous interpersonal interaction may be the least of the various evils that the participants have to choose from, or, more positively, the healthiest of the various transference-countertransference possibilities that are in the air at a certain time. It may be that such "healthier" types of interpersonal interaction actually do have something relatively new in them or maybe something with weak precursors in the patient's history that were not pathogenic but rather growth promoting. However, it is crucial that the therapist not assume this and that he be guided by the patient's subsequent associations in determining how the patient experienced the interaction and what it repeated or continued from the past.

Exploration of History in the Social Paradigm

An important weapon that the patient and the therapist have against prolonged deleterious forms of transference–countertransference enactment, in addition to the analyst's relative distance, is an evolving understanding of the patient's history. This understanding locates the transference–countertransference themes that are enacted in the analysis in a broader context that touches on their origins. This context helps immeasurably to free the patient and the analyst from the sense of necessity and importance that can become attached to whatever is going on in the here and now. The therapist's distance and ability to reflect critically on the process is aided by the fact that he, unlike the patient, does not reveal his private associations. The patient's ability to reflect on the process relies much more heavily on being able to explain what is happening on the basis of what has happened in the past. Such explanation, because it demonstrates how the patient's way of shaping and perceiving the relationship comes out of his particular history, also adds considerably to the patient's sense of conviction that alternative ways of relating to people are open to him. Again, what is corrected is not a simple distortion of reality but the investment that the patient has in shaping and perceiving his interpersonal experience in particular ways. Moreover, the past too is not explored in a spirit either of finding out what really happened (as in the trauma theory) or in the spirit of finding out what the patient, for internal reasons only, imagined happened (the past understood as fantasy). The patient as a credible (not accurate necessarily, but credible) interpreter of the therapist's experience has as its precursor the child as a credible interpreter of his parents' experience and especially his parents' attitudes toward himself (See Hartmann and Kris 1945, pp. 21-22; Schimek 1975, p. 180; Levenson, 1981). The dichotomy of environmentally induced childhood trauma and internally motivated childhood fantasy in etiological theories has its exact parallel in the false dichotomy in the psychoanalytic situation between reactions to actual countertransference errors on the analyst's part and the unfolding of pure transference which has no basis or only a trivial basis in reality.

The Patient's Perception of Conflict in the Analyst

The therapist's analytic task, his tendency toward understanding on the one hand, and his countertransference reactions on the other, often create a sense of real conflict as part of his total experience of the relationship. I think this conflict is invariably a part of what the patient senses about the therapist's response. In fact one subtle type of asocial conception of the patient's experience in psychoanalysis is one which implies that from the patient's point of view the analyst's experience is simple rather than complex, and unidimensional rather than multifaceted. The analyst is considered to be simply objective, or critical, or seductive, or threatened, or nurturant, or empathic. Any truly social conception of the patient's experience in psychoanalysis grants that the patient can plausibly infer a variety of more or less harmonious or conflictual tendencies in the analyst, some of which the patient would imagine were conscious and some of which he would think were unconscious. In such a model, the patient as interpreter understands that, however different it is, the analyst's experience is no less complex than his own.

REFERENCES

Benedek, T. (1953). Dynamics of the countertransference. *Bulletin of the Menninger Clinic* 17:201–208.
Bion, W. (1962). *Learning from Experience.* New York: Basic Books.
Bollas, C. (1983). Expressive uses of the countertransference. *Contemporary Psychoanalysis* 19:1–34.
Dewald, P. A. (1972). *The Psychoanalytic Process.* New York: Basic Books.
Ehrenberg, D. B. (1982). Psychoanalytic engagement. *Contemporary Psychoanalysis.* 18:535–555.

Fourcher, L. A. (1975). Psychological pathology and social reciprocity. *Human Development* 18:405-429.

Freud, S. (1912). The dynamics of transference. *Standard Edition* 12:99-108.

Gill, M. M. (1979). The analysis of the transference. *Journal of the American Psychoanalytic Association* 27:263-288.

——— (1982a) *Analysis of Transference I: Theory and Technique*. New York: International Universities Press.

——— (1982b) Merton Gill: an interview. *Psychoanalytic Review* 69:167-190.

——— (1983) The distinction between the interpersonal paradigm and the degree of the therapist's involvement. *Contemporary Psychoanalysis* 19:200-237.

Gill, M. M., and Hoffman, I. Z. (1982a). *Analysis of Transference II: Studies of Nine Audio Recorded Psychoanalytic Sessions*. New York: International Universities Press.

——— (1982b). A method for studying the analysis of aspects of the patient's experience of the relationship in psychoanalysis and psychotherapy. *Journal of the American Psychoanalytic Association* 30:137-167.

Greenson, R. (1965). The working alliance and the transference neurosis. *Psychoanalytic Quarterly* 34:155-181.

Hartmann, H., and Kris, E. (1945). The genetic approach to psychoanalysis. *Psychoanalytic Study of the Child* 1:11-30. New York: International Universities Press.

Heimann, P. (1950). On countertransference. *International Journal of Psycho-Analysis* 31:81-84.

Kohut, H. (1971). *The Analysis of the Self*. New York: International Universities Press.

——— (1977). *The Restoration of the Self*. New York: International Universities Press.

Levenson, E. (1981). Facts or fantasies: the nature of psychoanalytic data. *Contemporary Psychoanalysis* 17:486-500.

Lipton, S. D. (1977a). The advantages of Freud's technique as shown in his analysis of the Rat Man. *International Journal of Psycho-Analysis* 58:255-273.

——— (1977b). Clinical observations on resistance to the transference. *International Journal of Psycho-Analysis* 58:463-472.

——— (1982). A critical review of Paul Dewald's *The Psychoanalytic Process*. *Contemporary Psychoanalysis* 18:349-365.

Loewald, H. (1960). On the therapeutic action of psychoanalysis. *International Journal of Psycho-Analysis* 41:16–33.

Macalpine, I. (1950). The development of the transference. *Psychoanalytic Quarterly* 19:501–539.

Moore, B. E., and Fine, B. D. (1968). A *Glossary of Psychoanalytic Terms and Concepts.* New York: American Psychoanalytic Association.

Ogden, T. H. (1979). On projective identification. *International Journal of Psycho-Analysis* 60:357–373.

Racker, H. (1968). *Transference and Countertransference.* New York: International Universities Press.

Rogers, C. (1951). *Client-Centered Therapy.* Boston: Houghton Mifflin.

Sandler, J. (1976). Countertransference and role responsiveness. *International Review of Psycho-Analysis* 3:43–47.

_____ (1981). Character traits and object relationships. *Psychoanalytic Quarterly* 50:694–708.

Schimek, J. G. (1975). A critical re-examination of Freud's concept of unconscious mental representation. *International Review of Psycho-Analysis* 2:171–187.

Searles, H. F. (1975). The patient as therapist to his analyst. In *Tactics and Techniques in Psychoanalytic Theory,* ed. P. Giovacchini. New York: Jason Aronson.

_____ (1978–1979). Concerning transference and countertransference. *International Journal of Psychoanalytic Psychotherapy* 7:165–188.

Sterba, R. (1934). The fate of the ego in analytic therapy. *International Journal of Psycho-Analysis* 15:117–126.

Stone, L. (1961). *The Psychoanalytic Situation.* New York: International Universities Press.

Strachey, J. (1934). The nature of the therapeutic action of psychoanalysis. *International Journal of Psycho-Analysis* 15:117–126.

Szasz, T. (1963). The concept of transference. *International Journal of Psycho-Analysis* 44:432–443.

Tower, L. (1956). Countertransference. *Journal of the American Psychoanalytic Association* 4:224–255.

Wachtel, P. L. (1980). Transference, schema and assimilation: the relevance of Piaget to the psychoanalytic theory of transference. *The Annual of Psychoanalysis* 8:59–76.

Zetzel, E. R. (1956). Current concepts of transference. *International Journal of Psycho-Analysis* 37:369–376.

6

The Analysis of Transference[1]

Merton M. Gill

EDITOR'S SYNOPSIS

In a skillfully documented and carefully argued paper, Gill offers suggestions on how transference analysis may be improved. Citing work with transference as central to analytically informed technique, Gill asserts that it is not pursued as "systematically or comprehensively" as it could be. Distinguishing between resistance to transference awareness and resistance to transference resolution, Gill argues that insufficient attention is devoted to facilitating transference awareness, and that resolution of trans-

[1]This is a revised and expanded version of a paper read to the Chicago Psychoanalytic Society on May 23, 1978. It is a partial summary of a monograph. Its preparation was supported in part by Research Scientist Award, N.I.M.H. Grant #19436. Drs. Samuel D. Lipton, Irwin Hoffman, and Ilse Judas have helped me develop and clarify the ideas expressed in this paper. This paper was published in *Journal of the American Psychoanalytic Association*, 1979; 27:263–288.

ference must emphasize examination of the here-and-now interaction versus genetic investigation. Underemphasis of the here
and now is felt to be due to the fact that in vivo exploration of the
patient–therapist interaction has the potential of creating anxiety
in *both* patient and therapist. Both participants may thus be
motivated to avoid such interchange.

Gill stresses the importance of encouraging transference to
expand within the therapy and of increasing patient sensitivity
and willingness to discuss it. Patients may resist awareness and
discussion of transference reactions in that acknowledging here-
and-now affect is often uncomfortable. Feelings of a puzzling
and/or disturbing nature are difficult to disclose, particularly with
the very person toward whom they are directed. To expand
transference awareness Gill suggests the therapist view patient
associations regarding outside people and events as conveying
latent transference meaning. A patient's reactions to another, as
discussed in therapy, may pertain to the therapist as well. The
working assumption is that patient associations have implicit
transference implications and the therapist must listen with this
in mind.

In understanding transference reactions, Gill stresses attention to what in therapy may have served as a stimulus for the
patient's reaction. The therapist is seen as contributing to the
patient's transference; the concept of a pure transference reaction
unconnected to the present interaction is dismissed. It is asserted
that even the therapist's attempt to limit activity to create an
atmosphere where patient responses are largely determined by
his personal psychology cannot eliminate cues used to form
responses to the therapist. The therapist is cautioned that decreasing input to obtain unbiased transference material may elicit
a response based on the patient's perception of a withdrawn and
uninterested therapist. Gill emphasizes the importance of
viewing patient's reaction to therapist as plausible given the
information/cues the patient has. Giving credence to the patient's
ideas and striving to understand his reactions from his perspective are seen as critical in developing an atmosphere conducive to
productive exploration of transference.

Gill views here-and-now transference analysis as facilitating transference resolution in two ways. First, resolution is enhanced through identifying cues in the current relationship used by the patient as a point of departure for transference elaboration. Such cues are mutually assessed for their adequacy in stimulating the patient's response. If the stimulus is assessed as inadequate for the response, the patient is in a position to consider his interpretation of the situation. The patient is helped to see that the situation is subject to other possible interpretations and that the meaning he ascribes is not the only one available. Gill stresses that work is most productive when patient and therapist engage in a collaborative dialogue reflecting the stance that neither party has the total picture nor is there is an absolute way to perceive reality. A second way here-and-now analysis contributes to transference resolution is by providing a new experience for the patient. This new experience has two components. In here-and-now work the patient is treated differently than expected. The therapist's measured, curious, and investigative response differs from those responding wholeheartedly to the patient's transference provocation. In addition, the in vivo, here-and-now examination of interaction patterns is seen to offer an emotionally immediate and compelling opportunity to gain insight and consider change.

Gill's emphasis on the here and now, his illumination of patient and therapist resistance to this process, and his insightful views on how the patient may be productively engaged make for a seminal contribution to transference analysis. Echoing an analytical movement toward an interactional, interpersonal view of psychotherapy, his work merits careful study.

The analysis of the transference is generally acknowledged to be the central feature of analytic technique. Freud regarded transference and resistance as facts of observations, not as conceptual inventions. He wrote:

The theory of psychoanalysis is an attempt to account for two striking and unexpected facts of observation which emerge whenever an attempt is made to trace the symptoms of a neurotic back to their sources in his past life: the facts of transference and of resistance . . . Anyone who takes up other sides of the problem while avoiding these two hypotheses will hardly escape a charge of misappropriation of property by attempted impersonation, if he persists in calling himself a psychoanalyst. [1914a, p. 16]

Rapaport (1967) argued, in his posthumously published paper on the methodology of psychoanalysis, that transference and resistance inevitably follow from the fact that the analytic situation is interpersonal.

Despite this general agreement on the centrality of transference and resistance in technique, it is my impression, from my experience as a student and practitioner, from talking to students and colleagues, and from reading the literature, that the analysis of the transference is not pursued as systematically and comprehensively as I think it could be and should be. The relative privacy in which psychoanalysts work makes it impossible for me to state this view as anything more than my impression. On the assumption that even if I am wrong it will be useful to review issues in the analysis of the transference and to state a number of reasons that an important aspect of the analysis of the transference, namely, resistance to the awareness of the transference, is especially often slighted in analytic practice, I am going to spell out these issues and reasons in this paper.

I must first distinguish clearly between two types of interpretation of the transference. The one is an interpretation of resistance to the awareness of transference. The other is an interpretation of resistance to the resolution of transference. The distinction has been best spelled out in our literature by Greenson (1967) and Stone (1967). The first kind of resistance may be called defense transference. Although that term is mainly employed to refer to a phase of analysis characterized by a general resistance to the transference of wishes, it can also be used for a more isolated instance of transference of defense. The second kind of resistance is usually called transference resistance. With some oversimplification, one might say that in resistance to the awareness of transference, the transference is what is resisted, whereas in resistance to the resolution of transference, the transference is what does the resisting

Another more descriptive way of stating this distinction between resistance to the awareness of transference and resistance to the resolution of transference is between implicit or indirect references to the transference and explicit or direct references to the transference. The interpretation of resistance to awareness of the transference is intended to make the implicit transference explicit, while the interpretation of resistance to the resolution of transference is intended to make the patient realize that the already explicit transference does indeed include a determinant from the past.

It is also important to distinguish between the general concept of an interpretation of resistance to the resolution of transference and a particular variety of such an interpretation, namely, a genetic transference interpretation—that is, an interpretation of how an attitude in the present is an inappropriate carryover from the past. While there is a tendency among analysts to deal with explicit references to the transference primarily by a genetic transference interpretation, there are other ways of working toward a resolution of the transference. This paper will argue that not only is not enough emphasis being given to interpretation of the transference in the here and now, that is, to the interpretation of implicit manifestations of the transference, but also that interpretations intended to resolve the transference as manifested in explicit references to the transference should be primarily in the here and now, rather than genetic transference interpretations

A patient's statement that he feels the analyst is harsh, for example, is, at least to begin with, likely best dealt with not by interpreting that this is a displacement from the patient's feeling that his father was harsh but by an elucidation of some other aspect of this here-and-now attitude, such as what has gone on in the analytic situation that seems to the patient to justify his feeling or what was the anxiety that made it so difficult for him to express his feelings. How the patient experiences the actual situation is an example of the role of the actual situation in a manifestation of transference, which will be one of my major points.

Of course, both interpretations of the transference in the here and now and genetic transference interpretations are valid and constitute a sequence. We presume that a resistance to the transference ultimately rests on the displacement onto the analyst of attitudes from the past.

Transference interpretations in the here and now and genetic transference interpretations are of course exemplified in Freud's writings and are in the repertoire of every analyst, but they are not distinguished sharply enough.

Because Freud's case histories focus much more on the yield of analysis than on the details of the process, they are readily but perhaps incorrectly construed as emphasizing work outside the transference much more than work with the transference, and, even within the transference, emphasizing genetic transference interpretations much more than work with the transference in the here and now (see Muslin and Gill 1978). The example of Freud's case reports may have played a role in what I consider a common maldistribution of emphasis in these two respects—not enough on the transference and, within the transference, not enough on the here and now.

Before I turn to the issues in the analysis of the transference, I will only mention what is a primary reason for a failure to deal adequately with the transference. It is that work with the transference is that aspect of analysis that involves both analyst and patient in the most affect-laden and potentially disturbing interactions. Both participants in the analytic situation are motivated to avoid these interactions. Flight away from the transference and to the past can be a relief to both patient and analyst.

I divide my discussion into five parts: (1) the principle that the transference should be encouraged to expand as much as possible within the analytic situation because the analytic work is best done within the transference, (2) the interpretation of disguised allusions to the transference as a main technique for encouraging the expansion of the transference within the analytic situation, (3) the principle that all transference has a connection with something in the present actual analytic situation, (4) how the connection between transference and the actual analytic situation is used in interpreting resistance to the awareness of transference, and (5) the resolution of transference within the here and now and the role of genetic transference interpretation.

THE PRINCIPLE OF ENCOURAGING THE TRANSFERENCE TO EXPAND WITHIN THE ANALYTIC SITUATION

The importance of transference interpretations will surely be agreed to by all analysts, and the greater effectiveness of transference interpretations than interpretations outside the transference will be agreed to by many, but what of the relative roles of interpretation of the transference and interpretation outside the transference?

Freud can be read either as saying that the analysis of the transference is auxiliary to the analysis of the neurosis or that the analysis of the transference is equivalent to the analysis of the neurosis. The first position is stated in his saying (1913, p. 144) that the disturbance of the transference has to be overcome by the analysis of transference resistance in order to get on with the work of analyzing the neurosis. It is also implied in his reiteration that the ultimate task of analysis is to remember the past, to fill in the gaps in memory. The second position is stated in his saying that the victory must be won on the field of the transference (1912, p. 108) and that the mastery of the transference neurosis "coincides with getting rid of the illness which was originally brought to the treatment" (1917, p. 444). In this second view, he says that after the resistances are overcome, memories appear relatively without difficulty (1914b, p. 155).

These two different positions also find expression in the two very different ways in which Freud speaks of the transference. In "The Dynamics of Transference" (Chapter 1 in this volume), he refers to the transference, on the one hand, as *"the most powerful resistance* to the treatment" (1912, p. 101) but, on the other hand, as doing us "the inestimable service of making the patient's . . . impulses immediate and manifest. For when all is said and done, it is impossible to destroy anyone *in absentia* or *in effigie"* (1912, p. 108).

I believe it can be demonstrated that his principal emphasis falls on the second position. He wrote once, in summary: "Thus our therapeutic work falls into two phases. In the first, all the libido is forced from the symptoms into the transference and concentrated there; in the second, the struggle is waged around this new object and the libido is liberated from it" (1917, p. 455).

The detailed demonstration that he advocated that the transference should be encouraged to expand as much as possible within the analytic situation lies in clarifying that resistance is primarily expressed by repetition, that repetition takes place both within and outside the analytic situation, but that the analyst seeks to deal with it primarily within the analytic situation, that repetition can be not only in the motor sphere (acting) but also in the psychical sphere, and that the psychical sphere is not confined to remembering but includes the present, too.

Freud's emphasis that the purpose of resistance is to prevent remembering can obscure his point that resistance shows itself primarily by repetition, whether inside or outside the analytic situation: "The greater the resistance, the more extensively will acting out [repetition] replace remembering" (1914b, p. 151). Similarly in "The Dynamics of Transference" Freud said that the main reason that the transference is so well suited to serve the resistance is that the unconscious impulses "do not want to be remembered . . . but endeavour to reproduce themselves . . ." (1912, p. 108). The transference is a resistance primarily insofar as it is a repetition.

The point can be restated in terms of the relation between transference and resistance. The resistance expresses itself in repetition, that is, in transference both inside and outside the analytic situation. To deal with the transference, therefore, is equivalent to dealing with the resistance. Freud emphasized transference within the analytic situation so strongly that it has come to mean only repetition within the analytic situation, even though, conceptually speaking, repetition outside the analytic situation is transference too, and Freud once used the term that way:

We soon perceive that the transference is itself only a piece of repetition, and that the repetition is a transference of the forgotten past not only on to the doctor but also on to all the other aspects of the current situation. We . . . find . . . the compulsion to repeat, which now replaces the impulsion to remember, not only in his personal attitude to his doctor but also in every other activity and relationship which may occupy his life at the time . . . [1914b, p. 151]

It is important to realize that the expansion of the repetition inside the analytic situation, whether or not in a reciprocal relationship to repetition outside the analytic situation, is the avenue to control the repetition: "The main instrument . . . for curbing the patient's compulsion to repeat and for turning it into a motive for remembering lies in the handling of the transference. We render the compulsion harmless, and indeed useful, by giving it the right to assert itself in a definite field" (1914b, p. 154).

Kanzer has discussed this issue well in his paper on "The Motor Sphere of the Transference" (1966). He writes of a "double-pronged stick-and-carrot" technique by which the transference is fostered within the analytic situation and discouraged outside the analytic situation. The "stick" is the principle of abstinence as exemplified in the admonition against making important decisions during treatment, and the "carrot" is the opportunity afforded the transference to expand within the treatment "in almost complete freedom" as in a "playground" (Freud 1914b, p. 154). As Freud put it:

Provided only that the patient shows compliance enough to respect the necessary conditions of the analysis, we regularly succeed in giving all the symptoms of the illness a new transference meaning and in replacing his ordinary neurosis by a "transference neurosis" of which he can be cured by the therapeutic work. [1914b, p. 154]

The reason it is desirable for the transference to be expressed within the treatment is that there, it "is at every point accessible to our intervention" (1914b, p. 154). In a later statement he made the same point this way: "We have followed this new edition [the transference-neurosis] of the old disorder from its start, we have observed its origin and growth, and we are especially well able to find our way about in it since, as its object, we are situated at its very center" (1917, p. 444). It is not that the transference is forced into the treatment, but that it is spontaneously but implicitly present and is encouraged to expand there and become explicit.

Freud emphasized *acting* in the transference so strongly that one can overlook that repetition in the transference does not necessarily mean it is *enacted*. Repetition need not go as far as motor behavior. It can also be expressed in attitudes, feelings, and intentions, and, indeed, the repetition often does take such form rather than motor action. Such repetition is in the psychical rather than the motor sphere. The importance of making this clear is that Freud can be mistakenly read to mean that repetition in the psychical sphere can only mean remembering the past, as when he writes that the analyst

is prepared for a perpetual struggle with his patient to keep in the psychical sphere all the impulses which the patient would like to direct into the motor sphere; and he celebrates it as a triumph for the treatment if he can bring it about that something the patient wishes to discharge in action is disposed of through the work of remembering. [1914b, p. 153]

It is true that the analyst's effort is to convert acting in the motor sphere into awareness in the psychical sphere, but transference may be in the psychical sphere to begin with, albeit disguised. The psychical sphere includes awareness in the transference as well as remembering.

One of the objections one hears, from both analysts and patients, to a heavy emphasis on interpretation of associations about the patient's real life primarily in terms of the transference is that it means the analyst is disregarding the importance of what goes on in the patient's real life. The criticism is not justified. To emphasize the transference meaning is not to deny or belittle other meanings, but to focus on the one of several meanings of the content that is the most important for the analytic process, for the reasons I have just summarized.

Another way in which interpretations of resistance to the transference can be, or at least appear to the patient to be, a belittling of the importance of the patient's outside life is to make the interpretation as though the outside behavior is primarily an acting out of the transference. The patient may undertake *some* actions in the outside world as an expression of and resistance to the transference, that is, acting out. But the interpretation of associations about actions in the outside world as having implications for the transference need mean only that the choice of outside action to figure in the associations is codetermined by the need to express a transference indirectly. It is because of the resistance to awareness of the transference that the transference has to be disguised. When the disguised is unmasked by interpretation, it becomes clear that, despite the inevitable differences between the outside situations and the transference situation, the content is the same for the purpose of the analytic work. Therefore the analysis of the transference and the analysis of the neurosis coincide.

I stress this point particularly because some critics of earlier versions of this paper argued that I was advocating the analysis of the transference for its own sake rather than in the effort to overcome the neurosis. As I cited above, Freud wrote that the mastering of the transference neurosis "coincides with getting rid of the illness which was originally brought to the treatment" (1917, p. 444).

HOW THE TRANSFERENCE IS ENCOURAGED TO EXPAND WITHIN THE ANALYTIC SITUATION

The analytic situation itself fosters the development of attitudes with primary determinants in the past, that is, transferences. The analyst's reserve provides the patient with few and equivocal cues. The purpose of the analytic situation fosters the development of strong emotional responses, and the very fact that the patient has a neurosis means, as Freud said, that " . . . it is a perfectly normal and intelligible thing that the libidinal cathexis [we would now add negative feelings] of someone who is partly unsatisfied, a cathexis which is held ready in anticipation, should be directed as well to the figure of the doctor" (1912, p. 100).

While the analytic setup itself fosters the expansion of the transference within the analytic situation, the interpretation of resistance to the awareness of transference will further this expansion.

There are important resistances on the part of both patient and analyst to awareness of the transference. On the patient's part, this is because of the difficulty in recognizing erotic and hostile impulses toward the very person to whom they have to be disclosed. On the analyst's part, this is because the patient is likely to attribute the very attitudes to him that are most likely to cause him discomfort. The attitudes the patient believes the analyst has toward him are often the ones the patient is least likely to voice, in a general sense because of a feeling that it is impertinent for him to concern himself with the analyst's feelings, and in a more specific sense because the attitudes the patient ascribes to the analyst are often attitudes the patient feels the analyst will not like and be uncomfortable about having ascribed to him. It is for this reason that the analyst must be especially alert to the attitudes the patient believes he has, not only to the attitudes the patient does have toward him. If the analyst is able to see himself as a participant in an interaction, as I shall discuss below, he will become much more attuned to this important area of transference, which might otherwise escape him.

The investigation of the attitudes ascribed to the analyst makes easier the subsequent investigation of the intrinsic factors in the patient that played a role in such ascription. For example, the exposure of the fact that the patient ascribes sexual interest in him to the analyst, and genetically to the parent, makes easier the subsequent exploration of the patient's sexual wish toward the analyst, and genetically the parent.

The resistances to the awareness of these attitudes is responsible for their appearing in various disguises in the patient's manifest associations and for the analyst's reluctance to unmask the disguise. The most commonly recognized disguise is by displacement, but identification is an equally important one. In displacement, the patient's attitudes are narrated as being toward a third party. In identification, the patient attributes to himself attitudes he believes the analyst has toward him.

To encourage the expansion of the transference within the analytic situation, the disguises in which the transference appears have to be interpreted. In the case of displacement the interpretation will be of allusions to the transference in associations not manifestly about the transference. This is a kind of interpretation every analyst often makes. In the case of identification, the analyst interprets the attitude the patient ascribes to himself as an identification with an attitude he attributes to the analyst. Lipton (1977b) has recently described this form of disguised allusion to the transference with illuminating illustrations.

Many analysts believe that transference manifestations are infrequent and sporadic at the beginning of an analysis and that the patient's associations are not dominated by the transference unless a transference neurosis has developed. Other analysts believe that the patient's associations have transference meanings from the beginning and throughout. That is my opinion, and I think those who believe otherwise are failing to recognize the pervasiveness of indirect allusions to the transference—that is, what I am calling the resistance to the awareness of the transference.

In his autobiography, Freud wrote: "The patient remains under the influence of the analytic situation even though he is not directing his mental activities on to a particular subject. We shall be justified in assuming that nothing will occur to him that has not some reference to that situation" (1925, pp. 40–41). Since associations are obviously often not directly about the analytic situation, the interpretation of Freud's remark rests on what he meant by the "analytic situation."

I believe Freud's meaning can be clarified by reference to a statement he made in "The Interpretation of Dreams." He said that when the patient is told to say whatever comes into his mind, his associations become directed by the "purposive ideas inherent in the treatment" and that there are two such inherent purposive themes, one relating to the illness and the other—concerning which, Freud said, the patient has "no suspicion"—relating to the analyst (1900, pp. 531–532). If the patient has "no suspicion" of the theme relating to the analyst, the clear implication is that the theme appears only in disguise in the patient's associations. My interpretation is that Freud's remark not only specifies the themes inherent in the patient's associations, but also means that the associations are simultaneously directed by these two purposive ideas, not sometimes by one and sometimes by the other.

One important reason that the early and continuing presence of the transference is not always recognized is that it is considered to be absent in the patient who is talking freely and apparently without resistance. As Muslin and I pointed out in a paper on the early interpretation of transference (Gill and Muslin 1976), resistance to the transference is probably present from the beginning, even if the patient is talking apparently freely. The patient may well be talking about issues not manifestly about the transference that are nevertheless also allusions to the transference. But the analyst has to be alert to the pervasiveness of such allusions to discern them.

The analyst should proceed on the working assumption, then, that the patient's associations have transference implications pervasively. This assumption is not to be confused with denial or neglect of the current aspects of the analytic situation. It is theoretically always possible to give precedence to a transference interpretation if one can only discern it through its disguise by resistance. This is not to dispute the desirability of learning as much as one can about the patient, if only to be in a position to make more correct interpretations of the transference. One therefore does not interfere with an apparently free flow of associations, especially early, unless the transference threatens the analytic situation to the point where its interpretation is mandatory rather than optional.

With the recognition that even the apparently freely associating patient may also be showing resistance to awareness of the transference, the formulation that one should not interfere as long as useful information is being gathered should replace Freud's dictum that the transference should not be interpreted until it becomes a resistance (1913, p. 139).

CONNECTION OF ALL TRANSFERENCE MANIFESTATIONS WITH SOMETHING IN THE ACTUAL ANALYTIC SITUATION

As a prelude to a further discussion of the interpretive technique for expansion of the transference within the analytic situation, I will argue that every transference has some connection to some aspect of the current analytic situation. Of course all the determinants of a transference are current in the sense that the past can exert an influence only insofar as it exists in the present. What I am distinguishing is the current reality of the analytic situation, that is, what actually goes on between patient and analyst in the present, from how the patient is currently constituted as a result of his past.

All analysts would doubtless agree that there are both current and transferential determinants of the analytic situation, and probably no analyst would argue that a transference idea can be expressed without contamination, as it were, that is, without any connection to anything current in the patient–analyst relationship. Nevertheless, I believe the implications of this fact for technique are often neglected in practice. I will deal with them as my next point. Here I want only to argue for the connection.

Several authors (e.g., Kohut 1959, Loewald 1960) have pointed out that Freud's early use of the term *transference* in "The Interpretation of Dreams," in a connection not immediately recognizable as related to the present-day use of the term, reveals the fallacy of considering that transference can be expressed free of any connection to the present. That early use was to refer to the fact that an unconscious idea cannot be expressed as such, but only as it becomes connected to a preconscious or conscious content. In the phenomenon with which Freud was then concerned, the dream, transference took place from an unconscious wish to a day residue. In "The Interpretation of Dreams" Freud used the term *transference* both for the general rule that an unconscious content is expressible only as it becomes transferred to a preconscious or conscious content and for the specific application of this rule to a transference to the analyst. Just as the day residue is the point of attachment of the dream wish, so must there be an analytic-situation residue, though Freud did not use that term, as the point of attachment of the transference.

Analysts have always limited their behavior, both in variety and intensity, to increase the extent to which the patient's behavior is determined by his idiosyncratic interpretation of the analyst's behavior. In fact, analysts unfortunately sometimes limit their behavior so much, as compared with Freud's practice, that they even conceptualize the entire relationship with the patient a matter of technique, with no nontechnical personal relation, as Lipton (1977a) has pointed out.

But no matter how far the analyst attempts to carry this limitation of his behavior, the very existence of the analytic situation provides the patient with innumerable cues that inevitably become his rationale for his transference responses. In other words, the current situation cannot be made to disappear—that is, the analytic situation is real. It is easy to forget this truism in one's zeal to diminish the role of the current situation in determining the patient's responses. One can try to keep past and present determinants relatively perceptible from one another, but one cannot obtain either in "pure culture." As Freud wrote: "I insist on this procedure [the couch], however, for its purpose and result are to prevent the transference from mingling with the patient's associations imperceptibly, to isolate the transference and to allow it to come forward in due course sharply defined as a resistance" (1913, p. 134). Even "isolate" is too strong a word in the light of the inevitable intertwining of the transference with the current situation.

If the analyst remains under the illusion that the current cues he provides to the patient can be reduced to the vanishing point, he may be led into a silent withdrawal, which is not too distant from the caricature of an analyst as someone who does indeed refuse to have any personal relationship with the patient. What happens then is that silence has become a technique rather than merely an indication that the analyst is listening. The patient's responses under such conditions can be mistaken for uncontaminated transference when they are in fact transference adaptations to the actuality of the silence.

The recognition that all transference must have some relation to the actual analytic situation, from which it takes its point of departure, as it were, has a crucial implication for the technique of interpreting resistance to the awareness of transference, to which I turn now.

THE ROLE OF THE ACTUAL SITUATION IN INTERPRETING RESISTANCE TO THE AWARENESS OF TRANSFERENCE

If the analyst becomes persuaded of the centrality of transference and the importance of encouraging the transference to expand within the analytic situation, he has to find the presenting and plausible interpretations of resistance to the awareness of transference he should make. Here, his most reliable guide is the cues offered by what is actually going on in the analytic situation: on the one hand, the events of the situation, such as change in time of session, or an interpretation made by the analyst, and, on the other hand, how the patient is experiencing the situation as reflected in explicit remarks about it, however fleeting these may be. This is the primary yield for technique of the recognition that any transference must have a link to the actuality of the analytic situation, as I argued above. The cue points to the nature of the transference, just as the day residue for a dream may be a quick pointer to the latent dream thoughts. Attention to the current stimulus for a transference elaboration will keep the analyst from making mechanical transference interpretations, in which he interprets that there are allusions to the transference in associations not manifestly about the transference, but without offering any plausible basis for the interpretation. Attention to the current stimulus also offers some degree of protection against the analyst's inevitable tendency to project his own views onto the patient, either because of countertransference or because of a preconceived theoretical bias about the content and hierarchical relationships in psychodynamics.

The analyst may be very surprised at what in his behavior the patient finds important or unimportant, for the patient's responses will be idiosyncratically determined by the transference. The patient's response may seem to be something the patient as well as the analyst considers trivial, because, as in displacement to a trivial aspect of the day residue of a dream, displacement can better serve resistance when it is to something trivial. Because it is connected to conflict-laden material, the stimulus to the transference may be difficult to find. It may be quickly disavowed, so that its presence in awareness is only transitory. With the discovery of the disavowal, the patient may also gain insight into how it repeats a disavowal earlier in his life. In his search for the present stimuli that the patient is responding to transferentially, the analyst must therefore remain alert to both fleeting and apparently trivial manifest references to himself as well as to the events of the analytic situation.

If the analyst interprets the patient's attitudes in a spirit of seeing their possible plausibility in the light of what information the patient does have, rather than in the spirit of either affirming or denying the patient's views, the way is open for their further expression and elucidation. The analyst will be respecting the patient's effort to be plausible and realistic, rather than seeing him as manufacturing his transference attitudes out of whole cloth.

I believe it is so important to make a transference interpretation plausible to the patient in terms of a current stimulus that, if the analyst is persuaded that the manifest content has an important implication for the transference but he is unable to see a current stimulus for the attitude, he should explicitly say so if he decides to make the transference interpretation anyway. The patient himself may then be able to say what the current stimulus is.

It is sometimes argued that the analyst's attention to his own behavior as a precipitant for the transference will increase the patient's resistance to recognizing the transference. I believe, on the contrary, that, because of the inevitable interrelationship of the current and transferential determinants, it is only through interpretation that they can be disentangled.

It is also argued that one must wait until the transference has reached optimal intensity before it can be advantageously interpreted. It is true that too hasty an interpretation of the transference can serve a defensive function for the analyst and deny him the information he needs to make a more appropriate transference interpretation. But it is also true that delay in interpreting runs the risks of allowing an unmanageable transference to develop. It is also true that deliberate delay can be a manipulation in the service of abreaction rather than analysis and, like silence, can lead to a response to the actual situation, which is mistaken for uncontaminated transference. Obviously important issues of timing are involved. I believe an important clue to when a transference interpretation is apt and which one to make lies in whether the interpretation can be made plausibly in terms of the determinant I am stressing, namely, something in the current analytic situation.

A critic of an earlier version of this paper understood me to be saying that all that the analyst need do is to interpret the allusion to the transference, but that I did not see that interpretation of why the transference had to be expressed by allusion rather than directly is also necessary. Of course I agree, and meant to imply this as well as other aspects of the transference attitude in saying that when the analyst approaches the transference in the spirit of seeing how it appears plausibly realistic to the patient, it paves the way toward its further elucidation and expression.

THE RELATIVE ROLES OF RESOLUTION OF THE TRANSFERENCE WITHIN THE ANALYTIC SITUATION AND BY GENETIC TRANSFERENCE INTERPRETATION

Freud's emphasis on remembering as the goal of the analytic work implies that remembering is the principal avenue to the resolution of the transference. But his delineation of the successive steps in the development of analytic technique (1920, p. 18) makes clear that he saw this development as a change from an effort to reach memories directly to the utilization of the transference as the necessary intermediary to reaching the memories.

In contrast to remembering as the way the transference is resolved, Freud also described resistance as being primarily overcome in the transference, with remembering following relatively easily thereafter: "From the repetitive reactions which are exhibited in the transference we are led along the familiar paths to the awakening of the memories, which appear without difficulty, as it were, after the resistance has been overcome" (1914b, pp. 154–155); and

This revision of the process of repression can be accomplished only in part in connection with the memory traces of the process which led to repression. The *decisive* part of the work is achieved by creating in the patient's relation to the doctor—in the "transference"—new editions of the old conflicts. . . . Thus the transference becomes the battlefield on which all the mutually struggling forces should meet one another. [1917, p. 454; emphasis added]

This is indeed the primary insight Strachey (1934) clarified in his seminal paper on the therapeutic action of psychoanalysis.

There are two main ways in which resolution of the transference can take place through work with the transference in the here and now. The first lies in the clarification of what are the cues in the current situation that are the patient's point of departure for a transference elaboration. The exposure of the current point of departure at once raises the question of whether it is adequate to the conclusion drawn from it. The relating of the transference to a current stimulus is, after all, part of the patient's effort to make the transference attitude plausibly determined by the present. The reserve and ambiguity of the analyst's behavior is what increases the ranges of apparently plausible conclusions the patient may draw. If an examination of the basis for the conclusion makes clear that the actual situation to which the patient responds is subject to other meanings than the one the patient has reached, he will more readily consider his preexisting bias, that is, his transference.

Another critic of an earlier version of this paper suggested that, in speaking of the current relationship and the relation between the patient's conclusions and the information on which they seem plausibly based, I am implying some absolute conception of what is real in the analytic situation, of which the analyst is the final arbiter. That is not the case. My writing that what the patient must come to see is that the information he has is subject to other possible interpretations implies the very contrary to an absolute conception of reality. In fact, analyst and patient engage in a dialogue in a spirit of attempting to arrive at a consensus about reality, not about some fictitious absolute reality.

The second way in which resolution of the transference can take place within the work with the transference in the here and now is that in the very interpretation of the transference the patient has a new experience. He is being treated differently from how he expected to be. Analysts seem reluctant to emphasize this new experience, as though it endangers the role of insight and argues for interpersonal influence as the significant factor in change. Strachey's emphasis on the new experience in the mutative transference interpretation has unfortunately been overshadowed by his views on introjection, which have been mistaken to advocate manipulating the transference. Strachey meant introjection of the more benign superego of the analyst only as a temporary step on the road toward insight. Not only is the new experience not to be confused with the interpersonal influence of a transference gratification, but the new experience occurs together with insight into both the patient's biased expectation and the new experience. As Strachey points out, what is unique about the transference interpretation is that insight and the new experience take place in relation to the very person who was expected to behave differently, and it is this that gives the work in the transference its immediacy and effectiveness. While Freud did stress the affective immediacy of the transference, he did not make the new experience explicit.

It is important to recognize that transference interpretation is not a matter of experience, in contrast to insight, but a joining of the two together. Both are needed to bring about and maintain the desired changes in the patient. It is also important to recognize that no new techniques of intervention are required to provide the new experience. It is an inevitable accompaniment of interpretation of the transference in the here and now. It is often overlooked that, although Strachey said that only transference interpretations were mutative, he also said with approval that most interpretations are outside the transference.

In a further explication of Strachey's paper and entirely consistent with Strachey's position, Rosenfeld (1972) has pointed out that clarification of material outside the transference is often necessary to know what is the appropriate transference interpretation, and that both genetic transference interpretations and extratransference interpretations play an important role in working through. Strachey said relatively little about working through, but surely nothing against the need for it, and he explicitly recognized a role for recovery of the past in the resolution of the transference.

My own position is to emphasize the role of the analysis of the transference in the here and now, both in interpreting resistance to the awareness of transference and in working toward its resolution by relating it to the actuality of the situation. I agree that extratransference and genetic transference interpretations and, of course, working through are important too. The matter is one of emphasis. I believe interpretation of resistance to awareness of the transference should figure in the majority of sessions, and that if this is done by relating the transference to the actual analytic situation, the very same interpretation is a beginning of work to the resolution of the transference. To justify this view more persuasively would require detailed case material.

It may be considered that I am siding with the Kleinians who, many analysts feel, are in error in giving the analysis of the transference too great if not even an exclusive role in the analytic process. It is true that Kleinians emphasize the analysis of the transference more, in their writings at least, than do the general run of analysts. Indeed, Anna Freud's (1968) complaint that the concept of transference has become overexpanded seems to be directed against the Kleinians. One of the reasons the Kleinians consider themselves the true followers of Freud in technique is precisely because of the emphasis they put on the analysis of the transference. Hanna Segal (1967), for example, writes as follows:

To say that all communications are seen as communications about the patient's phantasy as well as current external life is equivalent to saying that all communications contain something relevant to the transference situation. In Kleinian technique, the interpretation of the transference is often more central than in the classical technique. [pp. 173–174]

Despite their disclaimers to the contrary, my reading of Kleinian case material leads me to agree with what I believe is the general view that Kleinian transference interpretations often deal with so-called deep and genetic material without adequate connection to the current features of the present analytic situation and thus differ sharply from the kind of transference interpretation I am advocating.

The insistence on exclusive attention to any particular aspect of the analytic process, like the analysis of the transference in the here and now, can become a fetish. I do not say that other kinds of interpretation should not be made, but I feel the emphasis on transference interpretations within the analytic situation needs to be increased or at the very least reaffirmed, and that we need more clarification and specification of just when other kinds of interpretations are in order.

Of course it is sometimes tactless to make a transference interpretation. Surely two reasons that would be included in a specification of the reasons for not making a particular transference interpretation, even if one seems apparent to the analyst, would be preoccupation with an important extratransference event and an inadequate degree of rapport, to use Freud's term, to sustain the sense of criticism, humiliation, or other painful feeling the particular interpretation might engender, even though the analyst had no intention of evoking such a response. The issue may well be, however, not of whether or not an interpretation of resistance to the transference should be made, but whether the therapist can find that transference interpretation that in the light of the total situation, both transferential and current, the patient is able to hear and benefit from primarily as the analyst intends it.

Transference interpretations, like extratransference interpretations, indeed like any behavior on the analyst's part, can have an effect on the transference, which in turn needs to be examined if the result of an analysis is to depend as little as possible on unanalyzed transference. The result of any analysis depends on the analysis of the transference, persisting effects of unanalyzed transference, and the new experience that I have emphasized as the unique merit of transference interpretation in the here and now. It is especially important to remember this lest one's zeal to ferret out the transference itself become an unrecognized and objectionable actual behavior on the analyst's part, with its own repercussions on the transference.

The emphasis I am placing on the analysis of resistance to the transference could easily be misunderstood as implying that it is always easy to recognize the transference as disguised by resistance or that analysis would proceed without a hitch if only such interpretations were made. I mean to imply neither, but rather that the analytic process will have the best chance of success if correct interpretation of resistance to the transference and work with the transference in the here and now are the core of the analytic work.

I close with a statement of a conviction designed to set this paper into a broader perspective of psychoanalytic theory and research. The points I have made are not new. They are present in varying degrees of clarity and emphasis throughout our literature. But like so many other aspects of psychoanalytic theory and practice, they fade in and out of prominence and are rediscovered again and again, possibly occasionally with some modest conceptual advance, but often with a newness attributable only to ignorance of past contributions. There are doubtless many reasons for this phenomenon. But not the least, in my opinion, is the almost total absence of systematic and controlled research in the psychoanalytic situation. I mean such research in contrast to the customary clinical research. I believe that only with such systematic and controlled research will analytic findings become solid and secure knowledge instead of being subject to erosion again and again by waves of fashion and what Ernst Lewy (1941) long ago called the "return of the repression" to designate the retreat by psychoanalysts from insights they had once reached.

SUMMARY

I distinguish between two major different relationships between transference and resistance. One is resistance to awareness of the transference and the other is resistance to resolution of the transference.

I argue that the bulk of the analytic work should take place in the transference in the here and now. I detailed Freud's view that the transference should be encouraged to expand within the analytic situation. I suggested that the main technique for doing so, in addition to the analytic setup itself, is the interpretation of resistance to the awareness of transference by searching for the allusions to the transference in the associations not manifestly about the transference; that in making such interpretations one is guided by the connection to the actual analytic situation that every transference includes; that the major work in resolving the transference takes place in the here and now, both by way of examining the relation between the transference and the actuality of the analytic situation from which it takes its point of departure and the new experience that the analysis of the transference inevitably includes; and that, while genetic transference interpretations play a role in resolving the transference, genetic material is likely to appear spontaneously and with relative ease after the resistances have been overcome in the transference in the here and now. Working through remains important, and it, too, takes place primarily in the transference in the here and now.

REFERENCES

Freud, A. (1968). Acting out. *Writings* 7:94–109. New York: International Universities Press, 1971.

Freud, S. (1900). The interpretation of dreams. *Standard Edition* 5.

—— (1912). The dynamics of transference. *Standard Edition* 12:99–108.

—— (1913). On beginning the treatment (Further recommendations in the technique of psychoanalysis, I). *Standard Edition* 12:123–144.

—— (1914a). On the history of the psycho-analytic movement. *Standard Edition* 14:7–66.

—— (1914b). Remembering, repeating, and working through (Further recommendations on the technique of psycho-analysis, II). *Standard Edition* 12:147–156.

—— (1917). Introductory lectures on psycho-analysis. *Standard Edition* 16.

—— (1920). Beyond the pleasure principle. *Standard Edition* 18:7–64.

—— (1925). An autobiographical study. *Standard Edition* 20:7–74. London: Hogarth, 1959.

Gill, M., and Muslin, H. (1976). Early interpretation of transference. *Journal of the American Psychoanalytic Association* 24:779–794.

Greenson, R. (1967). *The Technique and Practice of Psychoanalysis.* New York: International Universities Press.

Kanzer, M. (1966). The motor sphere of the transference. *Psychoanal. Quart.* 35:522–539.

Kohut, H. (1959). Introspection, empathy, and psychoanalysis. In *The Search for the Self,* pp. 205–232. New York: International Universities Press, 1978.

Lewy, E. (1941). The return of the repression. *Bull. Menninger Clinic* 5:47–55.

Lipton, S. (1977a). The advantages of Freud's technique as shown by his analysis of the Rat Man. *Internat. J. Psycho-Anal.* 58:255-274.
_____ (1977b). Clinical observations on resistance to the transference. *Internal. J. Psycho-Anal.* 58:463-472.
Loewald, H. (1960). On the therapeutic action of psychoanalysis. *Internal. J. Psycho-Anal.* 41:16-33.
Muslin, H., and Gill, M. (1978). Transference in the Dora case. *Journal of the American Psychoanalytic Association* 26:311-328.
Rapaport, D. (1967). The scientific methodology of psychoanalysis. In *Collected Papers*, ed. M. M. Gill, pp. 165-220. New York: Basic Books.
Rosenfeld, H. (1972). A critical appreciation of James Strachey's paper on the nature of the therapeutic action of psychoanalysis. *Internat. J. Psycho-Anal.* 53:455-462.
Segal, H. (1967). Melanie Klein's technique. In *Psychoanalytic Techniques*, ed. B. Wolman, pp. 168-190. New York: Basic Books.
Stone, L. (1967). The psychoanalytic situation and transference. *Journal of the American Psychoanalytic Association* 15:3-57.
Strachey, J. (1934). The nature of the therapeutic action of psychoanalysis. Reprinted in *Internat. J. Psycho-Anal.* (1969) 50:275-292.

SECTION II

RESISTANCE TO

HERE-AND-NOW WORK

Transference analysis is likely to be the most difficult aspect of psychological therapy for the analyst as well as the patient.

Merton Gill, 1991, p. 152[1]

Use of the immediate, here-and-now relationship to identify, explore, and resolve interpersonal conflict has support in the literature. Despite theoretical affirmation, here-and-now transference analysis is underemphasized in practice, often to the detriment of the therapy. Discrepancies between theory and practice are thought to derive from resistance in patient and therapist. Selected for inclusion in this section are papers that examine the nature of transference analysis and shed light on difficulties inherent to this process.

This section begins with a paper by Tarachow (1962) in

---

[1]Merton Gill, "Indirect Suggestion: A Response to Oremland's *Interpretation and Interaction*," *Interpretation and Interaction: Psychoanalysis or Psychotherapy* (Hillsdale, NJ: Analytic Press).

which he distinguishes between the "real" and "as if" relationship in psychotherapy. It is suggested that work with transference is compromised by object need in both patient and therapist. Difficulties in transference analysis often relate to the emotional wear-and-tear involved in focusing on the patient–therapist relationship, as opposed to outside relationships or one's past. The gratification attained in supportive therapy, or an expressive therapy without a transference focus, may be such that neither patient nor therapist may wish to subject their relationship to scrutiny. Maintaining a fully real and unexamined relationship may be a defense against the anxiety involved in its analysis. In the next paper Szasz (1963) approaches transference from a different angle. He argues that viewing the patient–therapist relationship as totally transference-derived may *also* be defensive, here against the impact of the patient's personality. The section concludes with a paper that I have coauthored (Bauer and Mills 1989). In this work a succinct description of here-and-now transference analysis is provided. Resistances of patient and therapist to this approach are detailed.

7

Interpretation and Reality in Psychotherapy[1]

Sidney Tarachow

EDITOR'S SYNOPSIS

A far-reaching work touching upon numerous therapeutic principles, this paper was chosen for the insight it provides regarding patient and therapist resistance to examining their relationship. While Tarachow distinguishes between psychoanalysis proper and psychotherapy, the reader is encouraged to consider Tarachow's comments regarding psychoanalysis as also applying to psychodynamic psychotherapy emphasizing transference analysis. Tarachow argues that for transference analysis to take place,

[1]Read at a meeting of the Psychoanalytic Association of New York on 19 March, 1962, in New York. This paper comprises sections of a book entitled *An Introduction to Psychotherapy*. The author is indebted to many colleagues for helpful discussions, comments, and ideas, particularly to Dr. Sylvan Keiser and to Dr. Richard Sterba for a most helpful correspondence. This paper was published in *The International Journal of Psycho-Analysis*, 1962; 43(6):377–387.

patient and therapist must set aside the gratification of relating to each other as real objects. The task of setting aside each other as real objects is regarded as the central problem in psychoanalysis. Both patient and therapist are faced with the basic problem of object need and are tempted to "live out" rather than examine their interaction. There is a wish in both to respond to each other as real objects and to regard their relationship as real.

Tarachow believes it is up to the therapist to take the initiative in transforming the real relationship into an analytic one. This is done by means of interpretation. The therapist's ability to examine and comment upon their relationship, and his encouragement of the patient to do so as well, transform the real situation into an analytic "as if" situation demanding scrutiny and comprehension. This transformation creates a state of tension, deprivation, and loneliness for both parties. To be helpful the therapist must be able to tolerate these affects, especially the loneliness. Tarachow asserts that the therapist will constantly be tempted to assuage this loneliness by treating the relationship with the patient as real.

While the principles underlying the "real" and "as if" relationship must be firmly grasped, it is acknowledged that they cannot be as sharply experienced in practice. It would be impossible to avoid a real relationship entirely, to view everything in an "as if" manner, as grist for the therapeutic mill. Nor would this be desirable in that aspects of the real relationship provide the patient needed motivation to face anxieties and do the work of therapy. Ironically, in the process of setting aside the patient as a real object the therapist offers a real relationship of a new and different sort. By examining and understanding versus acting in line with transference provocations, the therapist provides a different type of object relationship than has been previously experienced. This new relationship is viewed as helping the patient tolerate loss of his fantasy object (i.e., his infantile wishes toward others). The patient is assisted in abandoning his infantile objects by offering adult objects in exchange. Tarachow observes that without this incentive treatment of any kind would be dubious.

Tarachow's explication of object hunger, and of the inclination in both patient and therapist to seek unexamined interchange, provides illumination of a most basic resistance to here-and-now transference analysis. The affects inherent in the task of setting aside the other as real object may lead to its underemphasis or avoidance.

In an earlier paper in a panel on technique of psychoanalysis, I emphasized the problem of reality and the therapeutic task (Tarachow 1962). The point I emphasized then was the object need of *both* therapist and patient. For analysis to take place the need of one for another as a real object must be set aside. Another way of putting it would be to say that in the unanalysed transference the patient takes the therapist as real, and no analysis takes place. *The task of setting aside the other as a real object I regard as the central problem* in the theory of the treatment process. In this paper I wish to enlarge the theme, and also to place this conception within a larger framework that might serve as an overall conceptualization of all psychotherapeutic techniques as well as a conception of psychoanalysis.

I shall start with two introductory dimensions of the problem, first an elementary review of the task and goal of treatment, and second, definitions of psychoanalysis and psychotherapy. After this brief review I shall go on to the formulations offered for discussion.

Let us begin by saying that the patient has erected a barrier to the disorderly expression of his infantile and archaic wishes and drives. The barrier is his neurosis as well as his total personality, particularly his ego structure. We might also say that the total personality is a conglomeration of drive and defence. To speak in local clinical terms we might say that the obsessional neurosis is a barrier to and often a disguised gratification of archaic anality or anal sadism; depression is a barrier to and, in fantasy, the gratification of cannibalistic love-murder; hysteria is the barrier to and also the symbolic gratification of incestuous sexual wishes. The normal ego structure is the barrier to impatience and disorderliness. Both the normally functioning ego and the neurotic symptoms serve as a barrier; the tyro therapist should regard *both* as equally necessary for the patient, especially at the outset of treatment. Glover (1931) carefully cautions about this. We tend to underestimate the task we assign the patient, to set aside his hard-won ego defences. It must be added that the neurotic barriers become impediments to functioning, to happiness, and are often the sources of great mental pain. Even this must be qualified, since in some individuals the symptoms and compromises have so thoroughly found ego or superego approval that they have become inextricable and ego-syntonic elements of the total personality. Treatment with such individuals is often hopeless from the start.

The purposes of treatment are, first of all, to give the patient relief from suffering, and then to equip him better to live in peace, affection, and stable equilibrium with himself, his immediate objects, and the world as a whole. What design or plan is to be followed?

The therapist must assess the possibilities of intrapsychic change, the reality possibilities, the stability or precariousness of the balance of defences confronting him, the degree of change necessary or desirable, the minimum and maximum areas of intervention or susceptibility to interpretation or even confrontation, the size and regressed quality of the defences, the danger of eruption of powerful archaic feelings; make an estimate of the tolerance of insight, the risk of psychotic anxieties, the strength of the ego, its ability to form either new defences or new ego structures if insight or certain dislocations are attained. To arrive at this estimate, he must also consider the patient's age, sex, marital, financial, and occupational status, current success in life, talents, possibilities of sexual gratification, and, last but not least, favourable or adverse family constellations.

The therapist is now armed with the assessment and the therapeutic intention. The doctor–patient relationship, the transference and transference neurosis have to be added to our discussion. It may be decided that the patient can tolerate analysis, or that he can tolerate psychotherapy in various areas and to varying degrees. This decision leads directly to what the therapist will *permit* or *prevent* in the treatment relationship.

How can we state the treatment choice in terms that can be defined? There may be more than one definition. Suppose we define psychoanalysis and psychotherapy. Even the simplest definition demands consideration of the idea of the transference. Psychoanalysis would be that treatment in which the transference, repression, ego defences, and resistances are all freely subjected to analysis and resolved so far as may be required by the task of dealing with the infantile intrapsychic conflict and the derivative symptoms. Rangell (1954) has offered an excellent, comprehensive definition of psychoanalysis, but a briefer and more concise one seems preferable. My own definition would be even simpler: psychoanalysis is that treatment which takes into account the transference and the transference as a resistance. Of course, we have to know what the transference is. Some remarks on transference and transference neurosis will be made later.

Psychotherapy, on the other hand, is a selective, limited treatment in which the aim is a rearrangement rather than a resolution of these elements. The transference, repression, and resistances are dealt with in such a way that their stability is preserved, while trying at the same time to attain such of the analytic goals as are desirable or possible. We must search for psychoanalytic conceptions that will encompass all varieties of psychotherapy; we should be able to conceptualize even bad or unintended or spontaneous psychotherapy. The manoeuvres of psychotherapy are endless, but the conceptions underlying them should be simple and few.

Psychotherapies have been variously classified as (1) supportive, or (2) supportive with varying degrees of exploration and insight searching. Knight (1952) and Alexander (1954) have both offered similar divisions—supportive versus exploratory. We shall not discuss here the controversy over Alexander's idea that psychotherapy is a continuum and does not differ from analysis. Various principles of treatment are suggested for psychotherapy. In exploratory psychotherapy transference, resistance, and unconscious content are dealt with. Emphasis is placed, however, on setting limited goals (Knight 1952, Stone 1954). In turning to more specific technical measures, Coleman (1949) advised avoidance of intense dependency reactions, attention to current material, more active and more superficial interpretations, and limiting the duration of treatment. Stone (1954) emphasizes dealing with the realities of the patient's life, its daily events; the patient should be dealt with in his own idiom and attention should be centred on a selected few dynamic issues. My point of view about the instruction to pay attention to the reality issues of the psychotherapeutic patient would be to say that such instruction misses the central point. Attention is paid to reality in analysis as well as in psychotherapy. The difference is that in psychotherapy the real events are treated as *a reality*, while in analysis they are treated as expressions of the patient's fantasies and as determined by the inevitable needs of his solutions of his unconscious conflicts. This is a most important distinction; if the psychotherapist bears it in mind such specific instruction becomes unnecessary. Both Gill (1954) and Bibring (1954) give extensive instructions about what a psychotherapist should do, and classifications of what he does. The critical concern is the status and function of the relationship between therapist and patient. If it is taken as real, then the symptoms and life events are also taken as real, and both therapist and patient turn their backs on the unconscious fantasies and anxieties. If the real relationship is set aside, then both therapist and patient turn toward an understanding and working through of the unconscious fantasies.

I shall suggest three overriding principles of psychotherapy. Within these three principles any and all psychotherapeutic techniques should be comprehensible. The three are as follows:

1. Supply the infantile object in reality, that is, the unanalysed transference.
2. Supply displacements, that is, new symptoms and/or resistances.
3. Supply stability, that is, ego or superego building, or education, or reality events.

Any given technique may have the qualities of one or all of these three measures. On the first, that of supplying an object in reality, my remarks have been published in greater detail elsewhere (1962). The differences between psychoanalysis and psychotherapy were stated in terms of object relationship and loneliness. In analysis the analyst rejects the patient as object and teaches the patient (via analysis) to reject the analyst as object. Under such conditions problems are resolved by interpretation. In psychotherapy the therapist and patient retain each other as object, and varying areas of the patient's life remain uninterpreted, unanalysed. The two have entered each other's lives as real, serving as infantile objects to each other.

Nunberg (1951) distinguishes between psychoanalysis and psychotherapy in an almost identical way: "The psycho-analyst and the nonpsycho-analyst differ in their treatment of this phenomenon (transference) in that the former treats the transference symptoms as illusions while the latter takes them at face value, i.e., as realities." In psychotherapy the therapist actually intrudes into the life and personality of the patient and *stays there.* He offers himself as a new symptom. In an analysis the emphasis of the therapeutic process is the analysis of the transference as a resistance. In psychotherapy we regard the transference manifestations and their substructure as a vehicle for the cure in the sense that they are necessary building blocks for the patient's continued psychic functioning. The therapist uses himself as a building block in the oft-times jerry-built structure of defences that the patient has erected. In analysis this is (hopefully) resolved; in psychotherapy it is welcomed. What is resistance in analysis is a necessary permanent factor introduced into the patient's mental economy.

Glover (1960) gives an identical exposition of this idea:

The fact that the success of psycho-analytical techniques depends ultimately on the reduction of resistances tends to give rise to the mistaken impression that these defences are as pathological as the symptoms they are intended to conserve. On the contrary, the stability of normal

ego-formations is promoted to a considerable extent by psychic resistances to change. What is a stumbling block to psycho-analytical
technique is usually a pointer to the technique of non-analytical therapy.
In this sense the difference between psycho-analysis and general
psychotherapy is the difference between a mainly dynamic approach
and a mainly structural approach, in the one case reducing pathogenic
charges and in the other reinforcing the ego defences against pathogenic
charges.

The propositions I offer are as follows: both therapist and patient
face a basic problem, the problem of object need. In my terms this
basic object need is equivalent to Stone's (1961) "primal transference." I refer to an underlying and basic need for objects
independent of any specific neurotic structure and having no
specific relationship to any particular infantile projections. For
purposes of the discussion to follow it is not necessary to specify
whether it is a biological or psychological primary need (Balint
1952). In earliest life it is impossible to separate biological from
psychological needs. There is a need and a wish for a real object.
Every patient regards his therapist as real, regards all the manifestations of the treatment situation as real, and strives to regard
the therapist as a real object. The therapist, vis-à-vis the patient,
strives to do exactly the same. He, too, wants to regard the
patient as real and to respond to the patient as a real object. Thus,
both patient and therapist have a basic urge to mutual acting out.
    How is a therapeutic situation created out of this real
relationship between the two parties involved? It is created by an
act of the therapist. The therapist imposes a barrier to reality. We
shall here call it the therapeutic barrier. The imposition of this
barrier creates a therapeutic task for both therapist and patient.
The "real" situation is transformed into an "as if" situation
demanding attention and comprehension. The act that brings
about this transformation is interpretation. In a psychoanalysis
the same degree of task is imposed on both patient and therapist.
Nothing in the interaction is permitted to be regarded as real, and
everything is subjected to the scrutiny of both parties. Since the
initiative for the therapeutic barrier and therapeutic task comes

from the therapist we might grant that a greater degree of deprivation is imposed on him than on the patient. The degrees of severity of the task for both parties may vary sharply. In some cases the therapist may permit the patient a high degree of reality in his relationship to the therapist. For the therapist this might still be only a matter of technique, and to him the *as if* character of the patient will still be retained. The reference here to *as if* is not to be confused with the "as if" personality classically described by Helene Deutsch (1934). Her reference is to pathological identification without object relationship. In the context of this discussion the expression refers to a model interpretation, "You react 'as if' I were, etc., etc."

The degree of the barrier and task imposed on the patient may vary from patient to patient and from time to time, depending on the clinical needs of the moment and the long-term goals of the treatment effort. At one end of the scale is the rigorous psychoanalytic technique that makes the greatest demands of both. At the other end of the scale the entire relationship may be accepted as real, and the therapist may designedly enter all the phenomenology of the patient as a real object. This may be permitted to occur in some aspects of the treatment of psychoses, notably schizophrenia, and in the treatment of the young and certain acting out psychopaths. The need, in this sense, for another as object is neither transference nor countertransference. In our sense object need must first be *overcome* to establish the conditions for transference, or to be more precise, transference neurosis. *An uninterpreted relationship to the therapist is real, as real as any other relationship.* The interposition of the *as if* problem creates a state of tension and deprivation that is the kernel of the therapeutic task. The degree to which this task is imposed will depend on the therapist's evaluation of the patient's capabilities.

Interpretation interferes with reality and with the acting out of the unconscious fantasy. This increases the pressure of the unconscious fantasy and brings it forward into free association, or at least into progressive conflict with defensive forces that can be analysed. By this interference with acting out the real relationship is converted into a transference neurosis. The therapist has a choice: he may either join the patient in mutual acting out of the latter's unconscious fantasy, or he may act in such a way that the patient develops a transference neurosis. We might usefully differentiate between transference and transference neurosis. In a transference neurosis there is a distinct loss of reality sense, the patient is rigidly bound in his behavior by his projections onto the analyst, there is a strong preoccupation with the elements of the transference. In a sense the transference neurosis apparently directs the patient to reality, that is, to an interest in the analyst, but in another sense it is a highly narcissistic preoccupation. The patient is fixed to the unconscious fantasy that is being played out around the person of the analyst. The analyst's refusal to become a real object to the patient has thrust the latter back to his inner fantasy—has made him relatively more narcissistic, but has also made the fantasy material more available for scrutiny. This fantasy might be first available only in the form of acting out, but it is available to the discerning analyst. The analyst is confident enough of his own uninvolvement in the patient's fantasy to be able to take a neutral interpretive position to the phenomena. Under such conditions analysis can take place.

In conditions of transference that exist in psychotherapy such a state cannot be differentiated from an ordinary real relationship. The patient is permitted to act out his basic object needs as well as his infantile projections with the collusion of the therapist, to whatever degree the latter deems necessary for purposes of treatment. When the patient has accepted the therapist as object and when the therapist has assumed some importance to the patient we generally regard that as the establishment of transference. When the relationship assumes rigidly irrational characteristics and is determined by the fantasy and not by the real interplay between the two, that may be called transference neurosis.

The basic primary object need is present under all circumstances, although it might be obscured under the conditions of certain negative transference and transference-neurotic phenomena. These two—object need proper and special transference phenomena—should be regarded separately in the mind of the analyst.

The psychoanalyst must be capable of withstanding all degrees of the necessary deprivation, tension and task, especially requiring tolerance for loneliness. Winnicott (1958) makes some pertinent remarks referable to the capacity to be alone, which he characterizes as one of the most important signs of maturity. In essence he states that the ability to tolerate loneliness depends on previous childhood experience with an ego-supportive mother who has been introjected, making real reference to the actual mother unnecessary. It would follow that the analyst can tolerate *not* using the patient as object if his introjections and projections are based on affectionate and supportive rather than hostile relationships. Put in still another way, if the therapist is able basically to like and trust people he is also capable of the detachment necessary to treat them. The transference neurosis can be established only if the therapist can tolerate the isolation of not taking the patient as object. Loneliness is not to be regarded in a naive sense. A casual remark about the weather breaks the loneliness and establishes real object relationship.

Object relations arose at that unhappy moment of disruption of the symbiotic bond with mother. I would suggest that there are two primary techniques aimed at restoration of the symbiotic, pretraumatic bliss; one is identification, the other is object relationship. One is repair from the inside and the other repair from the outside, and both are forced upon us as reluctant necessities. At an early point in development there is not even too much difference between the two processes, as Freud (1923) reminds us in *The Ego and the Id*. The search for objects and the absolute necessity for objects remain with us for life. Ferenczi's (1950) second paper on the development of the sense of reality has a most interesting title,"The Problem of Acceptance of Unpleasant Ideas." Every new advance into reality is met by resistance and the effort to recreate the past as it had been before. All these well-known observations are repeated here simply to underscore the generic problem of the constant temptation to move close to objects, to have object relationships, to abandon mature ego differentiation for narcissistic and anaclitic object relationships, temptation to identification, and finally and basically for fusion. The therapist as well as the patient has a constant struggle against this array of temptations to come closer together. Margolin's (1953) reference to the blurred ego boundaries between patient and psychotherapist deals with precisely this point.

The therapeutic task for the therapist is his own struggle with his need for objects and with the self-imposed therapeutic barrier. The problem of spontaneous and unplanned acts of the analyst arises from this consideration. The temptation to breach the barrier will assail the therapist at all times. If the patient pleads for help he wants to extend himself; if the patient is hostile he wants to fight; if the patient is unhappy he wants to console him; if the patient is in need he wants to give. The therapist's task is to restrain himself from regarding these phenomena as real and thus destroying the transference "as if" potential. This restraint separates him from the patient as object and imposes upon him the task of tolerating loneliness. To complicate matters certain aspects of the treatment relationship *are* real, particularly certain of the masochistic aspects of the treatment situation as discussed by Menaker (1942). There are also certain real deprivations in the analytic process. To begin with, every interpretation is a deprivation. This is more so in some types of patients than others, especially for those who act out. Nevertheless every interpretation is designed to rob the patient of something, his fantasies, his defences, his gratifications. Analysis and, to varying extents, psychotherapy involve real disappointment.

An important deprivation is that the patient's assaults do not reach the therapist. The patient may express most intensely his love or his hatred, and what does the therapist do? He analyses it. It does not reach the analyst, and he does not care (so the patient thinks). This is a real defeat and reduction to childish impotence, which we expect our patients to tolerate lightly. We assist our patients to develop access to their real feelings, especially to the therapist, and then we refuse to treat these feelings as real. The patient is urged to treat his love for us as real, and we snub him for his pains. The very basis for an analysis involves *really* disappointing the patient. In psychotherapy we do not so completely disappoint the patient. This makes the therapist's role more bearable in psychotherapy than in analysis.

The course of an analysis might be summarized by saying that at the very outset the analyst denies himself the patient as a real object. The patient, on the other hand, begins therapy with the therapist as a real object and has slowly to learn to deny himself that gratification and so establish the necessary preconditions for the transference "as if." Mourning is a necessary part of treatment, not only as a termination problem, but from the very outset of treatment, from the very first interpretation. Just as the origins of thinking depend on the disruption of the symbiotic tie to mother and are connected with the first unpleasant idea (the first thought is an unpleasant one), so is there an analogous process in therapy. The therapeutic task can be imposed only by means of a disappointment and by transformation of a real into an "as if" relationship. We force thinking in place of reality: the uninterpreted relationship is reality.

There are certain types of relationships in which we are especially tempted to take the patient as a real object. Glover (1928, 1955) has some sage advice indeed. He wisely cautions the psychoanalyst to look out for the slightest alteration in his own behavior with any one or another of his patients. As soon as he notices any alteration he should look to himself. Under such circumstances the therapist has joined in collusion with the patient in taking some aspect of the patient's behavior as real and has responded to it in some real, nontherapeutic way. Spontaneous and unplanned remarks should be especially scrutinized, both the analyst's and the psychotherapist's. *The principal temptation is to play the role of mother.* The relief from the "as if" problem lends approval to the acceptance of the relationship to the therapist as real. In analysis this must be resolved; in psychotherapy it is helpful. If the therapist treats his patient as real he is using the patient to overcome his own sense of loneliness and sense of abandonment by his original symbiotic object. One's ego boundaries are the mark of one's disappointment and loneliness. There is a constant temptation and fear to break down these ego boundaries. This is the important anxiety that confronts the patient when he is required to free-associate. The most basic temptation between two individuals is the urge to regress in the character of object relations and to dissolve boundaries and fuse. Identification and object relations are not too far removed from symbiotic feelings and are an attempt to restore the symbiotic feeling.

It is a paradox that object relations, which we take as a mark of reality adjustment, are really designed to circumvent the painful recognition of reality. The extent of definite ego boundaries in normal object relations has been vastly overestimated. Healthy object relations permit and even demand periodic regressions and fusions, for example, carnivals, vacations, lovemaking. Schizophrenics show the most brittle and rigid ego boundaries of all. Schmideberg (1953) discusses this interesting point. Another paradox is that in the intimate successful therapeutic venture there is a real and close working together of two minds. How can this be reconciled with the therapeutic barrier and the therapeutic task? The special problem of the therapeutic situation is that we need real joint thinking to go on, but at the same time to prevent the union of the two individuals. How is this to be accomplished? We want to keep the barrier and still want the two to think *together*, not separately.

The answer to this apparent paradox is the specific act of the therapist. He demands the "as if" even at the moment of relaxed ego controls, or moment of regression, if you will. To meet this demand *both patient and therapist* must be capable of controlled ego splitting in the service of therapy. My impression is that the emphasis in the past has been on the necessity for the patient to be capable of ego splitting; I would add that the therapist, too, must have this capacity. Gill (1954) also makes this point. Psychoanalytic working through is analogous to mastery through play, play indulged in, though, by only part of the ego. Kardos and Peto (1956) discuss this in a similar way. So, in another context, does Sterba (1934). The problems are relived in an "as if" manner until they are understood, integrated, and no longer pathogenic. Sterba (1934) has discussed these problems in almost identical terms as, more recently, has Greenacre (1959). Sterba posited the need for a therapeutic dissociation of the ego of the patient. This would lead to two parts of the patient; one would form a therapeutic alliance with the analyst, and the other, the instincts and defences, would be set off at a distance to be understood and analysed. Sterba regards the analysis as a constant struggle to maintain this ego dissociation by means of interpretation. The object hunger of the patient is satisfied by the therapeutic alliance. He regards this latter satisfaction as an important function of transference. In spite of the remarkable similarity between the ideas of Sterba and those presented here, I regard the object hunger in a somewhat different light, and emphasize that this object hunger is as much a problem of the therapist as it is of the patient. This hunger must be set aside by both to establish the conditions for transference. In our view the uninterpreted relationship is real; the interpretation creates deprivation and transference. The pain of the neurosis is generally accepted as the motivation the patient brings with him to the analysis. The analyst introduces another motivation, the pain of the transference. This latter will shortly be subjected to further qualification.

In effective therapy there must be a capability of withdrawal from real object relations to guard the therapeutic task. A corollary of this would be that a real object relationship would involve a fusion of the two individuals to some degree. In therapy the withdrawal and fusion are both partial, hence ego splitting. In a therapeutic relationship both partners must be capable of the moment of loneliness. At least some part of the ego must be split off to perform the task of thinking and tolerating loneliness, to play with the experience and not live it, to think it and not live it. This is a difficult and time-consuming task; there are patients who not only regard the therapist-object as currently real, but to make things more difficult, even regard the past as currently real.

I have presented a rather rigorous conception of the ideal therapeutic relationship. The concept, that is, the concept of the conditions of analytic work, must be grasped firmly, but none of this can be experienced as sharply as I put it here. For example, in addition to the strictly controlled "as if" relationship there is also the real relationship. The patient gets to learn real things about his therapist both in and out of the office and the therapist behaves in a real and human way toward the patient (Glover 1955). In fact, the reality of the therapist is a factor that keeps the treatment going. The real relationship leads to identification, which also supplies motivation for the analytic work, for the ego splitting. The oscillation between the real and the "as if" relationship can actually facilitate analysis and, if considered in terms of oscillation between gratification and deprivation, can serve as a useful model for identification processes to take place. Seeing the therapist as he really is also assists the patient in correcting his transference distortions. In fact, it would probably be impossible to find any analyst who could rigorously maintain the detachment necessary not to use the patient as object at all. He would be bound to be real and treat the patient as real. Paradoxical as it may seem, the very human imperfections of the analyst make analysis possible in reality. Furthermore, it is the analyst's function to introduce reality to correct the patient's fantasies and distortions. The real relationship supplies the motivation to face the pain of the transference deprivations. In effect, there are two concurrent relationships, the real and the "as if." The very act of interpretation may have a double significance. What I have emphasized has been the function of interpretation in separating the patient and the therapist. But in another sense the interpretation brings the two together.

A paper by Garner (1961) raises some interesting and important theoretical questions about psychoanalysis and psychotherapy. He raises the question whether there is perhaps something basic in the treatment itself as distinct from the various and different psychoanalytic theories. His principal observation is that the passivity of the analyst is a fiction, and he goes on to indicate the aggressiveness and activity of the analyst. He points to the invitation to the patient to lie on the couch; the analyst's silence is regarded as an aggressive act; failure to gratify the patient is regarded as aggressive. He concludes that the common nonspecific elements of different types of treatment far outweigh the theoretical differences. One important element that Garner neglects to emphasize is the analyst's *demand* for free associations, a demand that the patient surrender his hard-won defences against painful ideas and affects. In psychotherapy there is of course no doubt of the activity of the psychotherapist. In terms of the conception of the object relationship between patient and therapist, what Garner is saying is that the common denominator of all therapies of whatever theoretical persuasion is the establishment of an object relationship, a sadomasochistic one. This object relationship has certain consequences. Even in the most classical analysis the object relationship cannot be avoided. What Garner is saying is that the establishment of an object relationship is more important than what specifically takes place in that object relationship. I accept Garner's emphasis, but would note that he does not carry his own conclusion far enough. All psychotherapists create real object relations with their patients; they establish a psychotherapeutic situation that can have clinically helpful results. The theoretical bias of the therapist *is* important, because this bias determines his attitude to the object relationship and to the changes in the patient as response. The relationship is a sadomasochistic one. Further implications of this type of relationship in the treatment process will be developed later, especially with regard to reassurance and neurotic worry.

I should like to turn to an immediate clinical implication of the problem of object relationship. What is the principal consequence of an interpretation? The principal consequence is object loss. A correct interpretation is followed by a mild depression. This is so whether the interpretation deals with the transference or with any other material. I had occasion to indicate to a patient that he wished I were his father. He agreed readily, but the interpretation left him tense and depressed. This was a patient with tenuous object relations, whose symptomatology involved a great deal of acting out. What he could not tolerate in my interpretation was the object loss involved. My interpretation implicitly demanded of him that he give me up as father. His continuing tension and depression required additional interpretation. The first interpretation now required a second interpretation concerning the object loss I was asking him to tolerate. So I said, "By my last remark I have refused to be your father." This made sense to him. The tension and depression vanished and was now replaced by unhappiness. He still wanted me to be his father. However, I had shown understanding of the sacrifice I was asking him to make and was taking the blame upon myself. This also helped the patient to reverse the direction of aggression within himself; his depression lifted. The point illustrated by this example is that an interpretation may require a second interpretation to deal with the loss of the object involved. Oddly enough the interpretation of the object loss might also be regarded as offering the patient something, in effect offering him a real object in this way in order to help him tolerate the loss of an object in another area. There is yet another way of putting it. We require the patient to abandon his infantile objects, and offer adult objects in exchange. Without this incentive perhaps no treatment of any kind would be possible. This could be a principle in education, too. After all, education is basically tolerance of pain and abandonment of pleasure. We cannot offer renunciation alone—we offer an object, generally the teacher.

I should like to make a further comment about the ego splitting necessary for the establishment of transference. In Nunberg's (1951) classic paper on transference and reality he described an interesting situation that he characterized as *readiness* for transference. He described a girl patient who wanted the analyst to change into a figure like her father. She did not *see* him as her father (which would have been a transference phenomenon); she badgered him to *change* into her father. Nunberg called this readiness for transference. I should regard this in a different way. It can be viewed as *resistance* to transference. This patient's treatment ended in failure. She was unable to tolerate the ego splitting necessary for the contemplation of the transference neurosis. She was unable to "play" the transference game. There are degrees of reality appreciation. In a true transference neurosis the patient misapprehends the analyst and regards certain phenomena as real and has certain wishes; when pressed the patient will detach himself and contemplate himself. Nunberg's patient had psychotic wishes and wanted no questioning of them.

This *resistance to transference* should not be confused with *transference as a resistance*. Transference as a resistance can be worked with analytically; in true transference there is a kind of turning to the analyst and a certain object relationship with the analyst. In the fully developed transference neurosis there are projections of the infantile object representations. There is also sufficient ego flexibility to tolerate a working ego split to contemplate this phenomenon. Nunberg's patient, although she seemed to demand that the analyst be her real object, had not really turned to the analyst. She was actually fixated to the original and real father, did not abandon that, and demanded that the analyst should step into her system and actually conform to her infantile object representations. This is a psychotic system, not even acting out. The analyst could not be interpreted to her *as* father, if he *is* father. She could not be persuaded to renounce one attachment in exchange for another, which is what we do in analysis. Nunberg also mentions that one of the fears of turning to the analyst is an anxiety about the passivity of doing so.

We now turn to the second area in the outline, supplying a displacement. For the theory of this measure I turn to Glover (1931) for his conception of "inexact interpretation." Glover distinguishes between an incomplete and an inexact interpretation. The incomplete interpretation is simply a step in correct analytic technique, in which the analyst gets the patient to move closer by degrees to the unconscious and/or infantile truth about himself. An inexact interpretation has a different purpose, even though at a given moment it might seem to be the same as the other. An inexact interpretation is offered as the definitive meaning of a certain arrangement of material, a meaning that, in the opinion of the analyst, actually falls short of the unconscious or infantile truth. The analyst has judged that the complete truth would be dangerous or intolerable to the patient. The patient seizes the inexact meaning eagerly because it helps him to continue to repress the truth; he can turn his back on the truth, and with the newly offered belief, in effect form a new symptom. In a sense the patient has been offered a benevolent phobia and eagerly grasps it. The real focus of the problem remains repressed and is displaced onto the given interpretation. This new symptom, the displacement, is the psychotherapeutic "cure." Glover correctly emphasizes that psychotherapy is on the side of defence.

Glover classifies nonanalytic techniques as follows: (1) ignore the truth altogether; turn away from the problem, "take a vacation"; (2) hypnosis or suggestion—this he characterizes as a transferred obsessional symptom; and (3) partial truth and suggestion.

In terms of my own outline the area of displacements can be broken down into four headings: (1) Displacement onto the transference. It is incompletely interpreted or not at all. (2) Displacement in the benign phobic sense, in the sense of Glover. (3) Projection. We might join the patient and blame the environment or specific people in the environment and neglect the intrapsychic conflicts that grew out of these outside factors, in effect establish a psychotherapeutic paranoia. (4) Introjection. We blame something within the body. The patient is treated medically. We help the patient to blame or attack his introjected objects, and along with the patient take these somatic symptoms as real, and not as derivatives of his unconscious intrapsychic conflicts. In the third and fourth directions we offer a delusion as a substitute for the presenting symptomatology. The *cost* is the sacrifice of knowledge of the truth; the *reward* is a functioning stability.

The concept of supplying displacements includes an entire array of manoeuvres in which the therapist selects the more ego-syntonic aspects of a problem and interprets only these, leaving the more troublesome factors undisturbed. In pathological marriages the heterosexual aspects might be dealt with. In pathological dependency relationships the libidinal aspects might be tolerable, but not the hatred or murderous feelings. In working with dreams, the manifest content or the immediate reality problem-solving aspects might be utilized. In passive-aggressive characters the aggressive wishes might be worked with, but the passivity might be gratified in the unanalysed transference relationship.

The third and last area in my outline is that of supplying stability. This might be done in a variety of ways. We might note in general that this also is in support of the defensive structures. Stability may be supplied by ego support or superego support. Id support would not be in the direction of stability; it would lead to difficulties. A patient scolded me for smiling at her in greeting. She accused me of insincerity and of stimulating her without promising her gratification. Ego support can be given by reality discussions of real events and by participation in decisions. A most important means of ego support is education and information. This enlarges the powers of the ego and so strengthens it. Education strengthens the ego but blocks fantasy. It contributes to stability, but interferes with access to the unconscious. Education strengthens resistances and defences. Education is restrictive in terms of the unconscious and is similar to inexact interpretation in terms of access to the unconscious. Any weakening of the ego might lead to a relapse into fresh symptomatology. Superego support is given by commands, prohibitions, and expressions of morals and moral values. Values are transmitted in a variety of ways, principally by the therapist's selection of which symptomatology he pursues and which he neglects. Changes in the environment might also contribute to stability.

One can turn to many authors in the literature and note how various techniques can all be understood in terms of the three general measures suggested: (1) to supply an object, (2) to supply displacements, and (3) to supply stability. Reider (1955) describes a fairly large number of cases either treated psychotherapeutically or spontaneously cured. Perhaps we can indicate the principle in each. He described a case helped by a hobby serving as an auxiliary defence. This patient was supplied with a new symptom. Another patient gave up alcohol on development of what was clearly a vicarious gratification of femininity—another new symptom. Another patient was helped by an ego-strengthening event to give up certain obsessions. Stability was supplied. These are cases of spontaneous cures. The dynamics are to be understood according to the same principles as in planned psychotherapy. Among cases of planned psychotherapy Reider describes the replacement of one symptom by another, the playing of a real role, the offering of controls to a patient, helping the patient stabilize a set of projections in the form of blaming the parents, and strengthening the defences. These can all be understood in terms of our scheme.

Repeatedly writers on psychotherapy insist, "Do not disturb the patient's defences, assist repression." This would certainly fall under the general heading of supplying stability. This can be done in many ways. Berliner (1941), in discussing a number of his cases of brief psychotherapy, indicates by a case example that psychotherapy should give the patient narcissistic satisfaction; in another case the therapist performs a mild superego function. These measures contribute to the stability of the mental apparatus by assisting the ego or superego. We might add that in some cases a weak ego might be assisted in its struggle with the power of the superego or the id. A certain degree of role playing might be necessary to effect this; a statement of values, morals, or judgements might even at times be necessary. Stability is thus supplied by ego building in one instance, superego strengthening in another, and mediation between superego and id in a third.

Reassurance is frequently suggested as a psychotherapeutic measure. The complications and dangers should be made clear. Reassurance is the assumption by the therapist of a real role in the patient's life. In one sense it fulfills the measure of supplying an object. However, this measure can also be understood more completely. Reassurance sets up a new sadomasochistic relationship between patient and therapist. It offers the patient a new, and on occasion dangerous, set of symptoms. The dangers are the risk of depression, masochistic fantasies, homosexual fantasies, or even paranoid ideas.

The sadomasochistic complications tempt me to make a tangential reference to neurotic worry. Worry is a comfortable defensive masochistic flight from extreme sadistic preoccupations. Worry is a masochistic defence against a sadistic object relationship. What does the therapist do when he reassures the worrying patient? He offers him a *new* sadomasochistic object relationship, but one in which the patient is now in the position of the helpless object. He has given him a new symptom from which he gains a degree of comfort and relief. Instead of being troubled by his drives to attack and by his superego tensions he has now been made the object of the therapist's attack; he is momentarily free from guilt and superego tension over his own sadistic drives. We relieve the patient by turning him into a victim. This, of course, brings its own complications.

Kindness should also be mentioned as an assault along with reassurance. A suggestion too would also be an assault. In fact, even an interpretation is an assault. Patients who have especially sensitive problems of passivity or latent homosexuality will become restless and angry or will even refuse to listen to an interpretation. How complete should an interpretation be? An interpretation should rarely go as far as possible. It should, by preference, fall short even of its immediate intended goal. This gives the patient an opportunity to extend the interpretation, gives him a greater share in the proceedings, and will to some extent mitigate the trauma of being the victim of help, of the therapist's approaches via interpretation.

The conception of "support" in psychotherapy deserves at least passing comment. Explicit verbal support has its dangers, as was discussed in connexion with reassurance and kindness. The most effective support is permitting oneself to be real to the patient in some implied or indirect way. A comment about the weather is sufficient to notify the patient that you are in his world and have not withdrawn into the distances of transference "as if." The patient then feels that he is not alone. Such indirect joining in the realities of the patient has the fewest dangers.

The character of termination of the treatment that the therapist accepts may also serve psychotherapeutic ends. A severely spiteful patient cannot acknowledge gratitude or obligation to anyone. He has been in treatment for a long time and has made many gains. He is faced by the difficulty of acknowledging that the therapist has helped him. He finds an excuse to become violently angry with the therapist and breaks off treatment. Under certain conditions this is an acceptable termination. The therapist makes no effort to acquaint the patient with his difficulties in loving the therapist. Another way of saying this is that the patient is permitted to end the treatment with the transference resistance at its height. This is precisely the reverse of the psychoanalytic goal. The therapist makes no effort to get the patient to confront his libidinal feelings. Contempt for the therapist becomes integrated into the feelings of independence. The therapist's narcissism must be sacrificed in the interests of the psychotherapeutic "cure." I certainly do *not* agree with Szurek (1958) that psychotherapy properly carried out must become psychoanalysis; this is a wholly unrealistic approach. Szurek underestimates the ego deformities, the weaknesses, the brittle defences, and the id resistances that so often make change impossible.

SUMMARY

The goal and task of treatment are stated.

Working definitions of psychoanalysis and psychotherapy are given. An outline of psychotherapeutic measures is suggested. There are three categories.

1. *Supply the infantile object.* This is the conception of the renunciation of the object in analysis and retention of the object in psychotherapy. The limitations, implications, and complications of this are discussed. This is the unanalysed transference.
2. *Supply or permit displacement.* This can take four directions:
   (a) to the transference
   (b) to new symptoms, via inexact interpretation
   (c) projection
   (d) introjection.

3. *Supply stability*. By way of
   (a) ego support
   (b) superego support
   (c) education and information
   (d) reality changes.

Certain related issues are also discussed, particularly the problem of motivation for treatment and the complications of reassurance.

REFERENCES

Alexander F. (1954). Psychoanalysis and psychotherapy. *J. Amer. Psychoanal. Assoc.* 2:722–733.

Balint, M. (1952). *Primary Love and Psychoanalytic Technique*. London: Hogarth.

Berliner, B. (1941). Short psychoanalytic psychotherapy: its possibilities and its limitations. *Bull. Menninger Clin.* 5:204–213.

Bibring, E. (1954). Psychoanalysis and dynamic psychotherapy. Similarities and differences. *J. Amer. Psychoanal. Assoc.* 2:745–770.

Coleman, J. V. (1949). The initial phase of psychotherapy. *Bull. Menninger Clin.* 13:189–197.

Deutsch, H. (1934). Uber einen Typus der Pseudoaffektivitat (als ob). *Int. Z. Psychoanal.* 20:323–335.

Ferenczi, S. (1950). The problem of acceptance of unpleasant ideas — advances in knowledge of the sense of reality. In *Further Contributions to the Theory and Technique of Psycho-Analysis*, pp. 366–379. London: Hogarth.

Freud, S. (1923). The ego and the id. *Standard Edition* 19.

Garner, H. H. (1961). Passivity and activity in psychotherapy. *Archives Gen. Psychiatry* 5:411–417.

Gill, M. M. (1954). Psychoanalysis and exploratory psychotherapy. *J. Amer. Psychoanal. Assoc.* 2:771–797.

Glover, E. (1928). The technique of psycho-analysis. Supplement No. 3. *Int. J. PsychoAnal.*

_____ (1931). The therapeutic effect of inexact interpretation: a contribution to the theory of suggestion. *Int. J. Psycho-Anal.* 12:397–411.

_____ (1955). *The Technique of Psychoanalysis*. New York: International Universities Press.

_____ (1960). Psycho-analysis and psychotherapy. *Brit. J. Med. Psychol.* 33:73–82.

Greenacre, P. (1959). Certain technical problems in the transference relationship. *J. Amer. Psychoanal. Assoc.* 7: 484–502.

Kardos, E., and Peto, A. (1956). Contributions to the theory of play. *Brit. J. Med. Psychol.* 29:100–112.

Knight, R. P. (1952). An evaluation of psychotherapeutic techniques. *Bull. Menninger Clin.* 16:113–124.

Margolin, S. (1953). Discussion in panel: the essentials of psychotherapy as viewed by the psychoanalyst. *J. Amer. Psychoanal. Assoc.* 1:550–561.

Menaker, E. (1942). The masochistic factor in the psychoanalytic situation. *Psychoanal. Quart.* 11:171–186.

Nunberg, H. (1951). Transference and reality. *Int. J. Psycho-Anal.* 32:1–9.

Rangell, L. (1954). Psychoanalysis and dynamic psychotherapy. Similarities and differences. *J. Amer. Psychoanal. Assoc.* 2:734–744.

Reider, N. (1955). Psychotherapy based on psychoanalytic principles. In *Six Approaches to Psychotherapy*, ed. J. L. McCary. New York: Dryden.

Schmideberg, M. (1953). Some clinical implications of the sense of bodily reality. *J. Hillside Hospital* 2:207–212.

Sterba, R. (1934). The fate of the ego in analytic therapy. *Int. J. Psycho-Anal.* 15:117–126.

Stone, L. (1954). The widening scope of psychoanalysis. *J. Amer. Psychoanal. Assoc.* 2:567–594.

_____ (1961). *The Psychoanalytic Situation. An Examination of its Development and Essential Nature.* New York: International Universities Press.

Szurek, S. A. (1958). *The Roots of Psychoanalysis and Psychotherapy.* Springfield, IL: Charles C Thomas.

Tarachow, S. (1962). Supervisors' conference: the problem of reality and the therapeutic task. *J. Hillside Hosp.* 11:21–28.

Winnicott, D. W. (1958). The capacity to be alone. *Int. J. Psycho-Anal.* 39:416–420.

8

The Concept of Transference[1]

Thomas S. Szasz

EDITOR'S SYNOPSIS

In this paper Szasz analyzes the meaning of transference and its role in psychoanalytic treatment. In early analytic work transference was viewed as a distortion of reality to be pointed out and clarified by the therapist. When conflicts of opinion arose, the therapist's judgment was most often considered correct (at least by the therapist) and reflecting reality; the patient's view was incorrect and reflecting transference. There are pitfalls in accepting the therapist's view as reality and the patient's as unreality. To Szasz, the designation of behavior as transference is a subjective judgment susceptible to bias and misinterpretation. What is transference and what is reality is not prelabelled; the therapist must do the labelling himself.

Though transference was traditionally treated as an idea

[1]This paper was published in The International Journal of Psycho-Analysis, 1963; 44: 432–443.

formed by the therapist regarding patient behavior, Szasz contends that it may express a judgment formed by the therapist *or* patient. There are four possible outcomes to this state of affairs. (1) The therapist and patient may agree the behavior is transference; the therapist can interpret and the patient may learn. (2) The therapist may consider it transference whereas the patient may not; here its analysis is precluded. (3) The therapist and patient may agree the behavior is not transference; this does not mean it is not. (4) The therapist may view the behavior as realistic whereas the patient knows it is not; the therapist cannot interpret but the patient may engage in a piece of self-analysis, usually after the session.

Szasz identifies an unrecognized function of the concept of transference, that of protecting the therapist from the impact of the patient's personality. The analytic situation is viewed as stimulating yet frustrating the development of an intense human relationship. Each participant is required to have a strong experience yet not act on it. How does the therapist protect himself from the impact of the patient's feelings? Szasz suggests that belief in transference enables the therapist to view patient feelings as not directed at him, but at the patient's internal objects. This permits a scientific detachment in an emotionally impactful situation. The therapist is afforded the emotional distance needed to consider how to respond without succumbing to the pressure of the moment. By attenuating the personal impact of the patient on the therapist, the concept of transference provides reassurance for the therapist. The behavior is not meant for him but others. The therapist functions as a symbolic substitute. Szasz, however, argues that the notion of "therapist as symbol" makes the "therapist as person" invulnerable. Undue emphasis on transference may serve to deny therapist countertransference and/or realistic, nondistorted patient perceptions. Herein lies a danger: just as the pre-Freudian therapist was too real to be effective, the analytic therapist may be too symbolic. Effective analysis requires the therapist to function as both.

Szasz's approach to transference is novel, stimulating, and instructive. His focus on the subjective nature of the transference interpretation highlights the importance of a collaborative, give-and-take interchange when processing the patient–therapist interaction. Neither party is privy to totally hard data regarding what transpires between them. The most helpful interpretations are those that are mutually authored. Szasz's elucidation of how the concept of transference may function as a therapist defense against overly intense involvement with the patient underscores the compelling impact a patient may have on the therapist. Therapist ability to constructively respond to this impact, steering a course between the Scylla of viewing one's relationship as "totally symbolic" and the Charybdis of establishing oneself as "fully real," may well determine the success of treatment.

A LOGICAL ANALYSIS

Transference is one of the most significant concepts in psychoanalysis. It is therefore especially important that its meaning be clear, and its use precise. In this essay, my aim is to present a brief analysis of the principal meanings and uses of this concept. This contribution is part of a larger effort whose aim is to identify those activities that are specifically psychoanalytic, and thus distinguish psychoanalysis from other forms of psychotherapy (Szasz 1957b, 1961).

Potentially, the subject of transference is as large as psychoanalysis itself. To make our task more manageable, I shall discuss transference under five separate headings as follows: (1) transference and reality, (2) transference in the analytic situation and outside it, (3) transference and transference neurosis, (4) transference as the analyst's judgement and as the patient's experience, (5) transference and learning.

Transference and Reality

Logically, transference is similar to such concepts as delusion, illusion, and phantasy: each is defined by contrasting it with "reality." Freud's (1914) classic paradigm of transference, it will be recalled, was the phenomenon of transference love—that is, the female patient's falling in love with the male therapist. Just what is this phenomenon? According to the patient, it is being in love with the analyst; according to Freud (1916–17), it is an illusion:

The new fact which we are thus unwillingly compelled to recognize we call *transference*. By this we mean a transference of feelings on to the person of the physician, because we do not believe that the situation in the treatment can account for the origin of such feelings. [p. 384]

We have encountered this distinction elsewhere: between imaginary and real pain, and between psychogenic and physical pain (Szasz 1957a). In these cases there is a conflict of opinion between patient and physician, which is not resolved by examination of the merits of the two views, but rather by the physician's autocratic judgement: his view is correct, and is considered "reality"; the patient's view is incorrect, and is considered "transference."

This idea is expressed by Nunberg (1951), when, in reply to the question, "What is transference?" he asserts:

Transference is a projection. The term *projection* means that the patient's inner and unconscious relations with his first libidinal objects are externalized. In the transference situation the analyst tries to unmask the projections or externalizations whenever they appear during the treatment. [p. 1]

This view is uncritically repeated in every discussion of the subject. The most trivial examples of "misidentification" are brought forward, again and again, as if they revealed something new. An excerpt from a recent paper by Spitz (1956) is illustrative:

Take the case of that female patient of mine who, after nearly a year's analysis with me, in connection with a dream, expressed the opinion that I was the owner of a head of rich, somewhat curly brown hair. Confronting her with the sorry *reality* made it easy to lead her to the insight that the proprietor of that tonsorial adornment was her father, and thus to achieve one little step in the clarification of her insight both in regard to the emotions she felt towards me and to those which she had originally felt towards her father. [p. 384, italics added]

On the face of it, there is nothing wrong with this account. But this is so only because the analyst's perception of the "facts" is so obviously more accurate than the patient's. This obscures the complexities and pitfalls inherent in the tactic of classifying the analyst's view as reality, and the patient's as unreality (Fenichel 1941). Here is a more challenging situation: the analyst believes that he is kindly and sympathetic, but the patient thinks that he is arrogant and self-seeking. Who shall say now which is "reality" and which "transference"? The point is that the analyst does not find the patient's reactions prelabelled, as it were; on the contrary, he must do the labelling himself. Hence, Nunberg's (1951) distinction between analytic and nonanalytic work does not help much:

The psycho-analyst and the non-psycho-analyst differ in their treatment and understanding of this phenomenon, in that the former treats the transference symptoms as *illusions* while the latter takes them at their face value, as realities. [p. 4, italics added]

There is no denying, however, that the distinction between transference and reality is useful for psychoanalytic work. But so is the distinction between real pain and imaginary pain for the work of the internist or the surgeon. Practical utility and epistemological clarity are two different matters. Workmanlike use of the concept of transference should not blind us to the fact that the term is not a neutral description but rather the analyst's judgement of the patient's behavior.

Transference in the Analytical Situation and Outside It

There has been much discussion in the psychoanalytic literature about the precise relation between transference and the analytic situation. Freud emphasized from the outset that man's tendency to form transferences is universal. Only the use we make of it is specific for analysis. Glover (1939) states this view succinctly:

As the transference develops, feelings originally associated with parental figures are displaced to the analyst, and the analytic situation is reacted to as an infantile one. The process of transference is of course not limited to the psycho-analytic situation. It plays a part and a useful part in all human relations whether with concrete objects (both animate and inanimate) or abstract "objects" (ideas). Hence, it is responsible for the most astonishing variations in the range of interest manifested by different individuals or by the same individual at different times. [p. 75]

Despite the clarity and simplicity of this view, many analysts have tried to redefine transference as a uniquely analytic phenomenon. Two classes of transferences are thus created: one analytic, the other nonanalytic.

Macalpine (1950) defines analytic transference as "a person's gradual adaptation by regression to the infantile analytic setting." Waelder (1956) also emphasizes the specificity of the analytic setting on the development of (analytic) transference:

Transference may be said to be an attempt of the patient to revive and re-enact, *in the analytic situation* and *in relation to the analyst*, situations and phantasies of his childhood. Hence transference is a regressive process. Transference develops *in consequence* of the conditions of the analytic experiment, viz., of the analytic situation and the analytic technique [p. 367, italics added]

Menninger (1958) limits transference to the analytic situation:

I define transference . . . as the unrealistic roles or identities unconsciously ascribed to a therapist by a patient in the regression of the psycho-analytic treatment and the patient's reactions to this representation derived from earlier experience. [p. 81]

This interpretation, and others like it, are perhaps efforts at being "operational"; but, if so, they overshoot the mark. To define transference in terms of the analytic situation is like defining microbes as little objects appearing under a microscope. The classic psychoanalytic position, exemplified by the writings of Freud, Fenichel, and Glover, though less pretentious, is more accurate. As the occurrence of bacteria is not limited to laboratories, so the occurrence of transference is not confined to the analytic situation; however, each is observed and studied best, not in its natural habitat, but under special circumstances.

This view does not imply that the analytic situation exerts no influence on the development of the transference. Of course it does. But so do all other situations in which transferences play a part, such as the doctor–patient relationship, marriage, the work situation, and so forth. The analytic relationship differs from all others in two ways: first, it facilitates the development of relatively intense transference reactions in the patient; second, it is a situation in which transferences are supposed to be studied and learned from, not acted upon.

Transference and Transference Neurosis

The difference between transference and transference neurosis is one of degree. Analysts generally speak of transferences when referring to isolated ideas, affects, or patterns of conduct that the patient manifests toward the analyst and that are repetitions of similar experiences from the patient's childhood; and they speak of transference neurosis when referring to a more extensive and coherent set of transferences (Hoffer 1956, Zetzel 1956).

The imprecision in this usage stems from a lack of standards as regards the quantity of transferences required before one can legitimately speak of a transference neurosis. In other words, we deal here with a quantitative distinction, but possess neither measuring instruments nor standards of measurement for making quantitative estimates. Thus, the distinction between transference and transference neurosis remains arbitrary and impressionistic.

Transference as the Analyst's Judgement and as the Patient's Experience

Traditionally, transference has been treated as a concept formed by the analyst about some aspect of the patient's conduct. For example, the female patient's declarations of love for the male analyst may be interpreted as unrealistic and due to transference. In this usage, the term *transference* refers to the analyst's judgement.

In addition, the word *transference* is often used, and indeed should be used, to describe a certain kind of experience that the analytic patient has, and that people in certain other situations may also have. The analytic patient may feel—with or without being told so by the analyst—that his love of the therapist is exaggerated; or that his hatred of him is too intense; or that his anxiety about the therapist's health is unwarranted. In brief, the patient may be aware that the therapist is "too important" to him. This phenomenon is what I mean by transference as experience and as self-judgement.

Although the experience of transference can never be completely absent from analysis—if it were, how could it be analysed?—it has been curiously neglected in the theory of psychoanalytic treatment.

Fenichel (1941) mentions it, but fails to elaborate on it:

Not everything is transference that is experienced by a patient in the form of affects and impulses during the course of an analytic treatment. If the analysis appears to make no progress, the patient has, *in my opinion*, the right to be angry, and his anger need not be a transference from childhood—or rather, we will not succeed *in demonstrating* the transference component in it. [p. 95, italics added]

The fact is that the analyst's judgement of whether or not the patient's behavior is transference may be validated by the patient; and conversely, the patient's experience and self-judgement may be validated by the analyst. Let us review briefly what such a process of cross-validation might entail.

To repeat, our premise is that the term *transference* expresses a judgement—formed either by the therapist or by the patient—about some aspects of the patient's behavior. Thus, a patient's action or feeling may be judged as (1) transference—if it is considered an expression of interest basically directed toward childhood objects, deflected to the analyst or to other figures in the patient's current life; or (2) reality-adapted behavior—if it is considered a valid feeling about, or reaction to, the person toward whom it is directed.

Since the analytic situation involves two persons, and since each has a choice of two judgements about any particular occurrence, there will be four possible outcomes:

1. Analyst and patient agree that the behavior in question is transference. This allows the analyst to interpret the transference, and the patient to experience it and learn from it.
2. The analyst considers the patient's behavior transference, but the patient does not. Instances of so-called transference love or erotized transference are illustrative. Regardless of who is correct, analyst or patient, such disagreement precludes analysis of the transference. The commonest reasons for this impasse are that the analyst is mistaken in his judgement, and that the patient, though exhibiting transference manifestations, is unaware of doing so.
3. Analyst and patient agree that the patient's behavior is reality-oriented. This calls for no work that is specifically analytic. Needless to say, in this case as in all the others, both analyst and patient may be mistaken.
4. The analyst may consider the patient's behavior realistic, but the patient may know it is transference. This possibility, at least in this form, is rarely discussed in psychoanalysis. Consistent with its neglect, there are no formal examples—like "transference love"—that could be cited to illustrate it. In general, the most common result is that the analyst "acts out." For example, he may engage in sexual

acts with the patient, when in fact the patient was only testing him; or he may give up analysing—believing that the patient is too depressed, suicidal, or otherwise unanalysable—when, again, the patient was merely "acting" difficult to test the analyst's perseverance in his efforts to analyse. This sort of occurrence cannot, of course, provide an opportunity for the analyst to make transference interpretations; it can, however, give the patient an opportunity to perform a piece of self-analysis, either during the analysis or, more often, afterwards.

The analyst outlined above helps to clarify the use of the word *transference* in the treatment of so-called borderline or schizophrenic patients (Winnicott 1956). In these cases, when analysts speak of transferences, they refer to constructions of their own that the patient does not share. On the contrary, to the patients, these experiences are invariably "real." The use of the term *transference* in this context might be valid; but it is not valid to speak of "analysing" such patients, because their so-called transferences can never be analysed (Szasz 1957c).

Transference and Learning

The patient's task in analysis is to discriminate between two aspects of his relationships: those based on transferences, and those based on reality. In other words, the patient must learn to distinguish his reactions to the analyst as a symbol and as a real person. The analytic relationship, if properly conducted, affords a particularly suitable—though not unique—situation for making this type of discrimination.

Phrased in terms of object relationships, we could say that the patient's task is to discriminate between the analyst as internal object and as external object. Internal objects can be dealt with only by intrapsychic defences; they can be tamed, but cannot be changed. To alter them, it is necessary to recognize the psychological existence of internal objects by their effects on actual, external objects. This can be accomplished only in the context of an actual human relationship. The analytic relationship—which allows the patient to invest the analyst with human qualities borrowed from others, but which the analyst neither accepts nor rejects, only interprets—is thus designed to help the patient learn about his internal objects. This sort of psychotherapeutic learning must be distinguished from other learning experiences, such as suggestion or imitation. Only a theory based on the educational model can accommodate the role of transference in psychoanlytic treatment.

Summary

1. The terms *transference* and *reality* are evaluative judgements, not simple descriptions of patient behavior.
2. Transferences occur in all human relationships. The analytic relationship differs from most others in (a) the ways in which it facilitates the development of transferences; and (b) the ways in which it deals with transference.
3. The distinction between transference and transference neurosis is quantitative and arbitrary; there is no standard of the amount of transference required for a transference neurosis.
4. Human behavior, especially in analysis, may be at once experienced and observed. Not only may the analyst consider the patient's behavior either "transference" or "reality," but so may the patient himself. The analyst can interpret only what he recognizes as transference; the patient can learn only from what he experiences as and himself considers transference.

THE CONCEPT OF TRANSFERENCE AS A DEFENCE FOR THE ANALYST

In the first part of my paper I have reviewed the role of the concept of transference in the theory of psychoanalytic treatment.

The aim of this second part is to demonstrate an unrecognized function of this concept: protecting the analyst from the impact of the patient's personality. In psychoanalytic *theory*, the concept of transference serves as an explanatory hypothesis, whereas in the psychoanalytic *situation*, it serves as a defence for the analyst. (Its function for the patient will not be considered in this essay.)

Types of Data in the Psychoanalytic Situation

It is often assumed, and sometimes stated, that the analyst's data are composed of the patient's verbal utterances and nonverbal behavior. Not only is this view seriously oversimplified, but completely false.

To begin with, we must distinguish between two different types of data available to the analyst—observation and experience. This is a familiar distinction; we are accustomed to speaking of the analysand's ego as being split into two parts, one experiencing, the other observing. This double ego-orientation, however, is not specific for analysis; most adults with adequately developed personalities, unless intensely absorbed in an experience, are capable of assuming both a concrete and an abstract attitude toward their actions and experiences (Goldstein 1951).

Even a solitary person, if self-reflective, has two classes of data about himself: first, his self-experience, for example, "I feel anxious"; second, his judgement of the experience: "It is silly, there is nothing to be afraid of."

In the analytic situation, the data—that is, who experiences, observes, and communicates what and to whom—are far more complex. The information available to the participants in a two-person situation may be arranged in a hierarchical fashion, as follows:

1. Each participant's own experience. (This is sometimes called "subjective experience," but the adjective is superfluous and misleading.)

2. Each participant's judgement of his experience; the observing ego takes its own experience as its object of study. For example, transference as an experience of the patient's, countertransference as an experience of the analyst's.
3. Each participant's judgement of his partner's experience. For example, the analyst's judgement that the patient's bodily experiences are hypochondriacal, or the patient's judgement that the analyst's friendliness is a facade.
4. Each participant's reaction to the partner's judgement of his experience. For example, the patient's reaction to the analyst's view that the patient is suffering from hypochondriasis, or the analyst's reaction to the patient's view that the analyst is the most understanding person in the world.
5. Logically, one reaction may be super-imposed on another, ad infinitum; in actuality, we can experience and comprehend only a few back and forth movements in this sort of communicational situation.

Let us apply these considerations to the problem of transference in the practice of psychoanalysis. To start with the simplest example: the analyst decides that a certain behavior by the patient is transference, and communicates this idea to him. The patient denies this, and claims that it is reality.

It is usually assumed that these two assertions contradict each other. Is this necessarily so? Only if each refers to the same object, occurrence, or relationship. This is the case when one person says, "Boston is east of New York," and another says, "No, Boston is west of New York." In many other situations, however, where apparently contradictory statements are uttered, attention to detail reveals that the two speakers are not talking about the "same thing." For example, a hypochondriacal patient may say to his physician, "I feel pains in my stomach"; the physician, having convinced himself that the patient is physically healthy, may counter with, "No, you don't have any pains, you are just nervous." These two people are talking about different things: the patient about his experiences, the physician about his medical judgement (Szasz 1957a). Both statements may be true; both may also be false.

The point is that when the analyst communicates to the patient the idea that the latter has transferences, he is expressing a judgement, whereas when the patient denies this, he may be communicating one of two things: his experience, or his judgement of his experience. In the first instance, there is no contradiction between analyst and patient: they are not talking about the same thing. Only when the patient's denial refers to his own judgement of his allegedly transferential behavior is there a contradiction between the assertions of the analyst and of the patient. But even then the two participants do not address themselves to and judge the "same object": the analyst addresses himself to the patient's behavior, whereas the patient addresses himself to (1) his own behavior as experience, plus (2) his judgement of his own behavior, plus (3) the analyst's interpretation of his behavior as transference.

I think we are justified in concluding that the analytic situation is not a setting in which clearly formulated logical propositions are asserted, examined, and accepted as true or rejected as false. What may appear in the analytic situation as logical contradiction may be resolved, by psychological and semantic analysis, into two or more noncontradictory propositions.

Transference as Logical Construct and as Psychological Defence

We are now ready for the thesis of this essay—namely, that although in psycho-analytic theory the main function of the concept of transference is to serve as a logical construct, in the psychoanalytic situation it is to serve as a psychological defence for the analyst. In other words, in the context of psychoanalytical treatment, transference has a specific *situational significance*, which is lost in the setting of a psychoanalytic journal or book. What is this specific role that the concept of transference plays in the analytic situation?

To answer this question, we must try to re-create the psychological mood of the analytic situation. It is, of course, a very intimate situation: two people meet alone, frequently, and over a long period of time; the patient discloses his most closely guarded secrets; and the analyst pledges to keep his patient's confidences. All this tends to make the relationship a close one. In technical terms, we say that the analyst becomes a libidinal object for the patient. But what is there to prevent the patient from becoming a libidinal object for the analyst? Not much. Patients do indeed become libidinal objects for analysts, up to a point. But if this were all that there was to analysis, the analytic relationship would not differ from that between trusted physician and patient, or legal adviser and client. What distinguishes the analytic relationship from all others is that patient as well as analyst are expected to make their relationship to each other an object of scientific scrutiny. How can they do this?

It is not as difficult as it is often made to seem. To begin with, the expectation of scrutiny of self and other is made explicit: the patient learns that it is not enough to immerse himself in the therapeutic relationship, and wait to be cured—as he might wait to have a tooth extracted. On the contrary, he is told (if he does not already know) that he must use to their utmost his powers of observation, analysis, and judgement. The analyst must do the same. We know, however, that human beings are not automatic thinking machines. Our powers of observation and analysis depend not only on our mental abilities, but also on our emotional state: powerful emotions are incentives to action, not to contemplation. When in severe pain, we want relief, not understanding of the causes of pain; when lonely, we want human warmth, not explanations of the causes of our loneliness; when sexually desirous, we want gratification, not rejection of our advances with the explanation that they are "transferences."

The analytic situation is thus a paradox: it stimulates, and at the same time frustrates, the development of an intense human relationship. In a sense, analyst and patient tease each other. The analytic situation requires that each participant have strong experiences, and yet not act on them. Perhaps this is one of the reasons that not only many patients, but also many therapists, cannot stand it; they prefer to seek encounters that are less taxing emotionally, or that offer better opportunities for discharging affective tensions in action.

Given this experientially intense character of the analytic encounter, the question is, how can the analyst deal with it? What enables him to withstand, without acting out, the impact of the patient's powerful feelings for and against him, as well as his own feelings for and against the patient? The answer lies in three sets of factors:

1. The personality of the therapist: he must be ascetic to an extent, for he must be able to bind powerful affects, and refrain from acting where others might not be able to do so.
2. The formal setting of analysis: regularly scheduled appointments in a professional office, payment of fees for services rendered, the use of the couch, and so forth.
3. The concept of transference: the patient's powerful affects are directed not toward the analyst, but toward internal objects.

In this essay, I shall discuss only the last element. The concept of transference serves two separate analytic purposes: it is a crucial part of the patient's therapeutic experience, and a successful defensive measure to protect the analyst from too intense affective and real-life involvement with the patient. For the idea of transference implies denial and repudiation of the patient's *experience qua experience*; in its place is substituted the more manageable construct of a *transference experience* (Freud 1914).

Thus, if the patient loves or hates the analyst, and if the analyst can view these attitudes as transferences, then, in effect, the analyst has convinced himself that the patient does not have these feelings and dispositions toward *him*. The patient does not really love or hate the analyst, but someone else. What could be more reassuring? This is why so-called transference interpretations are so easily and so often misused; they provide a ready-made opportunity for putting the patient at arm's length.

Recognizing the phenomenon of transference, and creating the concept, was perhaps Freud's greatest single contribution. Without it, the psychotherapist could never have brought scientific detachment to a situation in which he participates as a person. There is historical evidence, which we shall review presently, to support the thesis that this could not be done before the recognition of transference; nor, apparently, can it be done today by those who make no use of this concept.

Not only may the analyst use the concept of transference as a defence against the impact of the patient's relationship with him (as person, not as symbol), but he may also use the concept of a reality relationship with the patient as a defence against the threat of the patient's transferences! We see this most often in analysts who treat borderline or schizophrenic patients. Indeed, the defensive use of the reality relationship has become one of the hallmarks of the Sullivanian modification of psychoanalysis. There are good reasons for this.

In the analysis of the normal-neurotic individual, one of the great dangers to the therapist is a temptation: the patient may appear too inviting as a person, as a sexual object, and so forth. To resist this, convincing himself that the patient is not interested in him as a real person is eminently useful. In the therapy of the schizophrenic, however, one of the great dangers is compassion: the patient has suffered so horribly as a child that to recollect it might be too painful, not only for him but for the therapist as well. To counteract this danger, then, the therapist must convince himself that what the patient needs is not a review of his past misfortunes, but a good relationship with the therapist. This might be true in some instances; in others, it might be an example of the defensive use of the concept of a reality relationship (Szasz 1957c).

To recapitulate: I have tried to show that in the analytic situation the concepts of *transference* and *reality*—as judgements of the patient's behavior—may both be used defensively, one against the other. This phenomenon is similar to the defensive function of affects, for example of pain and anxiety: each may be used by the ego to protect itself from being overwhelmed by the other (Szasz 1957a).

The Reactions of Breuer and Freud to Eroticism in the Therapeutic Situation

The cathartic method, which was the precursor of analytic technique, brought out into the open the hysterical patient's ideas and feelings about herself and her "illness." This, in turn, led to the recognition of the patient's sexual feelings and needs.

So long as hysterical symptoms were undisturbed—or were only chased after with hypnosis—patients were left free to express their personal problems through bodily signs and other indirect communications. Indeed, the medical, including psychiatric, attitudes toward such patients invited them to continue this type of communicative behavior. Similarly, pre-Breuerian physicians were expected to respond to hysterical symptoms only in terms of their overt, common sense meanings: if a woman was neurasthenic, it was the physician's job to make her more energetic; if a man was impotent, he was to be made potent. Period. No other questions were to be asked. This state of affairs presented few problems to physicians (except that their therapeutic efficiency was low, but no lower than in organic diseases!), and led, of course, to no great changes in the patients. It was this *psychotherapeutically homeostatic situation between patients and doctors* that Breuer disturbed. He initiated the translation of the patient's hysterical body-language into ordinary speech (Szasz 1961).

But Breuer soon discovered that this was not at all like deciphering Egyptian hieroglyphics. The marble tablet remained unaffected by the translator's efforts, but the hysterical patient did not. Thus, as Breuer proceeded in translating Anna O.'s symptoms into the language of personal problems, he found it necessary to carry on a relationship with her without the protection previously afforded by the hysterical symptoms. For we ought not forget that the defences inherent in the hysterical symptoms (and in others as well) served not only the needs of the patient, but also of the physician. So long as the patient was unaware of disturbing affects and needs—especially aggressive and erotic—she could not openly disturb her physician with them. But once these inhibitions were lifted—or, as we might say, once the translation was effected—it became necessary for the therapist to deal with the new situation: a sexually aroused attractive *woman*, rather than a pitifully disabled *patient*.

Breuer, as we know, could not cope with this new situation, and fled from it. Freud, however, could, and thereby established his just claim to scientific greatness.

My foregoing comments are based on the many historical sources of the origins of psychoanalysis made available to us, especially in the past decade. Instead of citing specific facts, most of which are familiar to analysts, I shall quote some passages from Jones's (1953) biography of Freud, which illustrate how the need for transference as a defence for the therapist arose, and the function it served for Breuer and Freud.

Freud has related to me a fuller account than he described in his writing of the peculiar circumstances surrounding the end of this novel treatment. It would seem that Breuer had developed what we should nowadays call a strong counter-transference to his interesting patient. At all events he was so engrossed that his wife became bored at listening to no other topic, and before long jealous. She did not display this openly, but became unhappy and morose. It was a long time before Breuer, with his thoughts elsewhere, divined the meaning of her state of mind. It provoked a violent reaction in him, perhaps compounded of love and guilt, and he decided to bring the treatment to an end. He announced this to Anna O., who was by now much better, and bade her good-bye. But that evening he was fetched back to find her in a greatly excited state, apparently as ill as ever. The patient, who according to him had appeared to be an asexual being and had never made any allusion to such a forbidden topic throughout the treatment, was now in the throes of an hysterical childbirth (pseudocyesis), the logical termination of a phantom pregnancy that had been invisibly developing in response to Breuer's ministrations. Though profoundly shocked, he

managed to calm her down by hypnotizing her, and then fled the house
in a cold sweat. The next day he and his wife left for Venice to spend a
second honeymoon, which resulted in the conception of a daughter; the
girl born in these circumstances was nearly sixty years later to commit
suicide in New York.

Confirmation of this account may be found in a contemporary
letter Freud wrote to Martha, which contains substantially the same
story. She at once identified herself with Breuer's wife, and hoped the
same thing would not ever happen to her, whereupon Freud reproved
her vanity in supposing that other women would fall in love with *her*
husband: "for that to happen one has to be a Breuer."

The poor patient did not fare so well as one might gather from
Breuer's published account. Relapses took place, and she was removed
to an institution in Gross Enzerdorf. A year after discontinuing the
treatment, Breuer confided to Freud that she was quite unhinged and
that he wished she would die and so be released from her suffering. She
improved, however, and gave up morphia. A few years later Martha
relates how "Anna O.," who happened to be an old friend of hers and
later a connection by marriage, visited her more than once. She was
then pretty well in the daytime, but still suffered from her hallucinatory
states as evening grew on.

Frl. Bertha (Anna O.) was not only highly intelligent, but extremely attractive in physique and personality; when removed to the
sanatorium she inflamed the heart of the psychiatrist in charge. Her
mother, who was somewhat of a dragon, came from Frankfurt and took
her daughter back there for good at the end of the eighties. Bertha, who
was born and brought up in Vienna, retained her Viennese grace,
charm, and humour. Some years before she died she composed five
witty obituary notices of herself for different periodicals. A very serious
side, however, developed when she was thirty, and she became the first
social worker in Germany, one of the first in the world. She founded a
periodical and several institutes where she trained students. A major
part of her life's work was given to women's causes and emancipation,
but work for children also ranked high. Among her exploits were several
expeditions to Russia, Poland, and Roumania to rescue children whose
parents had perished in pogroms. She never married, and she remained
very devoted to God.

Some ten years later, at a time when Breuer and Freud were
studying cases together, Breuer called him into consultation over an

hysterical patient. Before seeing her he described her symptoms, whereupon Freud pointed out that they were typical products of a phantasy pregnancy. The recurrency of the old situation was too much for Breuer. Without saying a word he took up his hat and stick and hurriedly left the house. [pp. 224–226]

I should like to underscore the following items in this account:

1. Having effected the translation from hysterical symptom directed impersonally to anyone, to sexual interest directed to the person of Breuer himself, Breuer panicked and fled. The relationship evidently became too intense for him.
2. Breuer protected himself from the danger of this relationship—that is, from his anxiety lest he succumb to Anna O.'s charms—first, by literally fleeing into the arms of his wife, and later by convincing himself that his patient was "very sick," and would be better off dead!
3. Freud, to whom Anna O.'s problem was essentially a theoretical one—he had no personal, therapeutic relationship with her—dealt with the threat of a too intense involvement with female patients by convincing himself that this could happen only to Breuer. I shall comment on this later.

Let us now take a look at the events preceding the publication of *Studies on Hysteria* (1893–95).

In the late eighties, and still more in the early nineties, Freud kept trying to revive Breuer's interest in the problem of hysteria or to induce him at least to give to the world the discovery his patient, Frl. Anna O., had made. In this endeavour he met with a strong resistance, the reason for which he could not at first understand. Although Breuer was much his senior in rank, and fourteen years older, it was the younger man who—for the first time—was entirely taking the leading part. It gradually dawned on Freud that Breuer's reluctance was connected with his disturbing experience with Frl. Anna O. related earlier in this chapter.

So Freud told him of his own experience with a female patient suddenly flinging her arms around his neck in a transport of affection, and he explained to him his reasons for regarding such untoward occurrences as part of the transference phenomena characteristic of certain types of hysteria. This seems to have had a calming effect on Breuer, who evidently had taken his own experience of the kind more personally and perhaps even reproached himself for indiscretion in the handling of his patient. At all events Freud ultimately secured Breuer's cooperation, it being understood that the theme of sexuality was to be kept in the background. Freud's remark had evidently made a deep impression, since when they were preparing *Studies* together, Breuer said apropos of the transference phenomenon, "I believe that is the most important thing we both have to make known to the world." [Jones 1953, p. 250]

In this account, the following facts deserve emphasis:

1. The psychotherapeutic material on which Freud discovered transference concerned not his own patient, but someone else's: the experiences were Anna O.'s and Breuer's, the observations Freud's.
2. A heavy thread of denial runs through Freud's thinking in formulating the concept of transference; for example, for it to happen, " . . . one has to be a Breuer"; when he found that one does not, he concluded that the patient's love transference is due to the nature of the hysterical illness—under no circumstances must the patient's attraction to the therapist be considered "genuine."
3. Freud's concept of transference was vastly reassuring to Breuer.

We shall examine each of these topics in greater detail.

Transference as a Defence for the Analyst

Anna O., Breuer, and Freud

The fact that Anna O. was not Freud's patient has, I think, not received the attention it deserves. Possibly, this was no lucky accident, but a necessary condition for the discovery of the basic insights of psychoanalysis. In other words, the sort of triangular situation that existed between Anna O., Breuer, and Freud may have been indispensable for effecting the original breakthrough for dealing scientifically with certain kinds of highly charged emotional materials; once this obstacle was hurdled, the outside observer could be dispensed with.

It seems highly probable that Freud's position vis-à-vis both Breuer and Anna O. helped him assume a contemplative, scientific attitude toward their relationship. Breuer was an older, revered colleague and friend, and Freud identified with him. He was thus in an ideal position to empathize with Breuer's feelings and thoughts about the treatment of Anna O. On the other hand, Freud had no significant relationship with Anna O. He thus had access to the kind of affective material (from Breuer) that had been unavailable to scientific observers until then; at the same time, he was able to maintain a scientific attitude toward the data (which impinged upon him only by proxy).

It is sometimes said that the psychoanalytic method was discovered by Anna O. Actually, she discovered only the cathartic method and—as it turned out—its limited therapeutic usefulness. She was, however, a truly important collaborator in a more important discovery: the concept of transference. This concept is the cornerstone of psychoanalytic method as well as theory, and was created through the delicate collaboration of three people—Anna O., Breuer, and Freud. Anna O. possessed the relevant basic facts; Breuer transformed them into usable scientific *observations*, first by responding to them in a personal way, and second by reporting them to Freud; Freud was the *observer* and *theoretician*.

Subsequently, Freud succeeded in uniting the latter two functions in himself. In his self-analysis, he was even able to supply all three roles from within the riches of his own personality. It is unfortunate that Freud's self-analysis is sometimes regarded as a uniquely heroic achievement. To be sure, he might have been the first person ever to perform this sort of work (although one cannot be sure of this); he was certainly the first to describe and thus make public the methods he used. The discovery of Newton's laws and the principles of calculus were also heroic achievements; this does not prevent us from expecting high school students to master them and, indeed, to go beyond them. There is no reason to treat psychoanalysis differently.

To repeat: I have tried to show that because Anna O. was not Freud's patient it was easier for him to assume an observing role toward her sexual communications than if they had been directed toward himself.

Denial and Transference

Let us now examine Freud's attempt to reassure his fiancée, by writing her that female patients could fall in love "only with a Breuer," never with him.

Freud may have believed this to be true, or if not, he may have thought it would reassure Martha; or, he may have toyed with both possibilities, believing now one, now the other. The evidence for the probability of each of these hypotheses, though only suggestive, is worth pondering.

We must start with a contradiction: Freud asserted that female hysterical patients have a "natural" tendency to form love transferences toward their male therapists; if so, one surely does not have to be a Breuer for this to happen. But then why did he write to Martha as he did?

We can only guess. Perhaps it was, as already mentioned, merely a device to reassure his fiancée. He might have done this, however, more effectively by explaining his concept of transference to her; it was, as we know, very reassuring to Breuer. There may have been two reasons why he did not do this. First, his concept of transference was perhaps not as clearly formulated when he wrote to Martha in 1883, as when he used it on Breuer nearly ten years later. Second, Freud was under the influence of a powerful, positive father transference to Breuer. From this point of view, Freud's assertion that women fall in love "only with a Breuer" assumes new importance. It means that Breuer is the father, Freud the son. Thus, his statement to Martha would mean that women fall in love only with fathers (adult males), not with children (immature boys).

I mention these things, not to analyse Freud, but to cast light on the function of the concept of transference for the analyst. Freud's self-concept during the early days of psychoanalysis is relevant to our understanding of the work-task of the analyst. His self-depreciating remark is appropriate to the reconstruction offered above of the triangular relationship of Anna O., Breuer, and Freud. It seems that Freud had divided certain activities and roles between Breuer and himself: Breuer is the "father," the active therapist, the heterosexually active male; Freud is the "son," the onlooker or observer, the sexually inactive child. This, let us not forget, was the proper social-sexual role of the middle-class adolescent and young adult in the Vienna of the 1880s; aware of sexual desire, he was expected to master it by understanding, waiting, working, and so forth. The same type of mastery—not only of sexual tensions, but of all other kinds that may arise in the analytic situation—must be achieved by the analyst in his daily work.

When Freud was young—and presumably sexually most able and most frustrated—it may have been easier for him to believe that sexual activity with his female patients was impossible, than that it was possible but forbidden. After all, what is impossible does not have to be prohibited. A saving of defensive effort may thus be achieved by defining as impossible what is in fact possible.

Denial plays another role in the concept of transference. For, in developing this concept, Freud denied, and at the same time reaffirmed, the reality of the patient's experience. This paradox, which was discussed before, derives from the distinction between experience and judgement. To deny what the patient felt or said was not new in psychiatry; Freud carried on this tradition, but gave it a new twist.

According to traditional psychiatric opinion, when a patient asserts that he is Jesus Christ, the psychiatrist ought to consider this a delusion. In other words, what the patient says is treated as a logical proposition about the physical world; this proposition

the psychiatrist brands as false. Psychiatrists and nonpsychia-
trists alike, however, have long been aware that the patient may,
indeed, feel as though he were Jesus Christ, or be convinced that
he is the Saviour; and they may agree with the fundamental
distinction between affective experiences about the self and
logical propositions about the external world. The epistemological
aspects of this problem, and their relevance to psychiatry, were
discussed elsewhere (Szasz 1961; and the first part of this paper).
What is important to us now is to recognize that, in the concept
of transference, Freud introduced this fundamental distinction
into psychiatry, without, however, clarifying the epistemological
foundation of the concept.

Thus, when Freud introduced the concept of transference
into psychiatry, he did not deny the patient's self-experience: if
the patient declares that she is in love with the analyst, so be it.
He emphatically repudiated, however, the action-implication of
the experience: the patient's "love" must be neither gratified nor
spurned. In the analytic situation, both of these commonsénse
actions are misplaced; in their stead Freud offered "analysis"
(Freud 1914). He thus took what modern philosophers have come
to describe as a *meta position* toward the subject before him
(Reichenbach 1947).

Transference and Reassurance

The notion of transference is reassuring to therapists precisely
because it implies a denial (or mitigation) of the "personal" in the
analytic situation. When Freud explained transference to Breuer,
Breuer drew from it the idea that Anna O.'s sexual overtures were
"really" meant for others, not for him; he was merely a symbolic
substitute for the patient's "real" love objects. This interpretation
reassured Breuer so much that he dropped his objections to
publishing *Studies on Hysteria*.

The concept of transference was needed by Freud, no less
than by Breuer, before either dared publish the sort of medicopsy-
chological material never before presented by respectable scientists. The reaction of many medical groups confirmed Breuer's

fears: this type of work was a matter for the police, not for doctors. More than just the prudery of German medical circles of the late nineteenth century is betrayed by this view; it suggests that, in psychoanalysis, what stands between obscenity and science is the concept of transference. This concept, and all it implies, renders the physician a nonparticipant with the patient in the latter's preoccupation with primary emotions (such as eroticism, aggression, etc.). Only by not responding to the patient on his own level of discourse and instead analysing his productions, does the analyst raise his relationship with the patient to a higher level of experience. Unable to comprehend the meaning of transference, Freud's early critics could not distinguish analytic work from indecent behavior.

The concept of transference was reassuring for another reason as well. It introduced into medicine and psychology the notion of the *therapist as symbol*; this renders the *therapist as person* essentially invulnerable.

When an object becomes a symbol (of another object) people no longer react to it as an object; hence, its features qua object become inscrutable. Consider the flag as the symbol of a nation. It may be defiled, captured by the enemy, even destroyed; national identity, which the flag symbolizes, lives on nevertheless.

The concept of transference performs a similar function: the analyst is only a symbol (therapist), for the object he represents (internal imago). If, however, the therapist is accepted as symbol—say, of the father—his specific individuality becomes inconsequential. As the flag, despite what happens to it, remains a symbol of the nation, so the analyst, regardless of what he does, remains a symbol of the father to the patient. Herein lies the danger. Just as the pre-Freudian physician was ineffective partly because he remained a fully "real" person, so the psychoanalyst may be ineffective if he remains a fully "symbolic" object. The analytic situation requires the therapist to function as both, and the patient to perceive him as both. Without these conditions, "analysis" cannot take place.

The use of the concept of transference in psychotherapy thus led to two different results. On the one hand, it enabled the analyst to work where he could not otherwise have worked; on the other, it exposed him to the danger of being "wrong" vis-à -vis his patient—and of abusing the analytic relationship—without anyone being able to demonstrate this to him.

If we agree that there is such an inherent error in psychoanalysis—and it is hard to see how anyone could dispute this today—it behooves us to try to correct it. Of course, there have been many suggestions, beginning with Freud's proposal that analysts should undergo a personal analysis, and ending with the current emphasis on so-called high standards in analytic institutes. All this is futile. No one, psychoanalysts included, has as yet discovered a method to make people behave with integrity when no one is watching. Yet this is the kind of integrity that analytic work requires of the analyst.

Summary

My aim in this part of my essay has been to develop the thesis that the concept of transference fulfils a dual function: it is a logical construct for the psychoanalytic theoretician, and a psychological defence for the psychoanalytic therapist. To illustrate and support this thesis, the historical origins of the concept were reexamined. Breuer, it appears, was overcome by the "reality" of his relationship with Anna O. The threat of the patient's eroticism was effectively tamed by Freud when he created the concept of transference; the analyst could henceforth tell himself that he was not the genuine object, but a mere symbol, of his patient's desire.

Transference is the pivot upon which the entire structure of psychoanalytic treatment rests. It is an inspired and indispensable concept; yet it also harbours the seeds, not only of its own destruction, but of the destruction of psychoanalysis itself. Why? Because it tends to place the person of the analyst beyond the reality testing of patients, colleagues, and self. This hazard must be frankly recognized. Neither professionalization, nor the "raising of standards," nor coerced training analyses can protect us from this danger. Only the integrity of the analyst and of the analytic situation can safeguard from extinction the unique dialogue between analysand and analyst.

REFERENCES

Fenichel, O. (1941). *Problems of Psychoanalytic Technique.* (Albany, NY: Psychoanalytic Quarterly.

Freud, S. (1914). Observations on transference-love (Further Recommendations on the Technique of Psycho-Analysis, III). *Standard Edition* 12.

_____ (1916–1917). *A General Introduction to Psychoanalysis.* Garden City, NY: Garden City Publishing Company, 1943.

Glover, E. (1939). *Psycho-Analysis. A Handbook for Medical Practitioners and Students of Comparative Psychology.* London: Staples, 1949.

Goldstein, K. (1951). *Human Nature in the Light of Psychopathology.* Cambridge, MA: Harvard University Press.

Hoffer, W. (1956). Transference and transference neurosis. *Int. J. Psycho-Anal.* 37.

Jones, E. (1953). *The Life and Work of Sigmund Freud.* Vol. I. London: Hogarth.

Macalpine, I. (1950). The development of the transference. *Psychoanal. Quart.* 19.

Menninger, K. (1958). *The Theory of Psychoanalytic Technique.* New York: Basic Books.

Nunberg, H. (1951). Transference and reality. *Int. J. Psycho-Anal.* 32.

Reichenbach, H. (1947). *Elements of Symbolic Logic.* New York: Macmillan.

Spitz, R. A. (1956). Transference: the analytic setting and its prototype. *Int. J. Psycho-Anal.* 37.

Szasz, T. S. (1957a). *Pain and Pleasure: A study of Bodily Feelings.* New York: Basic Books.

_____ (1957b). On the theory of psycho-analytic treatment. *Int. J. Psycho-Anal.*, 38.

_____ (1957c). A contribution to the psychology of schizophrenia. *A.M.A. Arch. Neurol. Psychiat.* 77.

_____ (1961). *The Myth of Mental Illness. Foundations of a Theory of Personal Conduct.* New York: Hoeber/Harper.

Waelder, R. (1956). Introduction to the discussion on problems of transference. *Int. J. Psycho-Anal.* 37.

Winnicott, D. W. (1956). On transference. *Int. J. Psycho-Anal.* 37.

Zetzel, E. (1956). Current concepts of transference. *Int. J. Psycho-Anal.* 37.

9

Patient and Therapist Resistance to Use of the Transference in the Here and Now[1]

Gregory P. Bauer and John A. Mills

EDITOR'S SYNOPSIS

This paper was chosen for its concise depiction of transference analysis and of resistances to it that exist in patient and therapist. The authors contend that early trends in psychoanalytic intervention emphasized understanding the genesis of conflict. Of late there has been considerable interest in a more active analysis and working through of disturbed patterns of relatedness as they are expressed in the therapeutic dyad. This approach, termed the *analysis of transference in the here and now,* highlights use of the patient–therapist interaction to identify, examine, and modify interpersonal conflict.

    The notion of a more active, here-and-now approach to transference is not new. Seminal figures such as Rank, Ferenzci, Reich, Sullivan, and, more recently, Davanloo have all stressed such work. Despite theoretical support, there are important

[1]This paper was published in *Psychotherapy,* 1989; 26(1):112–119.

discrepancies between theory and practice. These discrepancies are thought to stem from resistances in patient and therapist that inhibit effective work in the here and now.

Difficulties that interfere with the patient's ability to productively examine transference include the following: (1) The patient's perception that a focus on the here-and-now relationship is at the expense of "presenting problems" or reality concerns. (2) Anxiety accompanying self-disclosure, which may make it difficult for the patient to reveal his or her feelings for the therapist. The patient may deny their existence or discount their importance. (3) The patient's belief that his or her feelings are based on the "person" of the therapist and have no "transference" basis, even when the patient is willing to discuss reactions to the therapist. The conclusion the patient wants to believe is that there is no blind repeating of the past. (4) Examination and modification of transference patterns, which may be resisted because such work obliges the patient to squarely face one's problems, the role one has in bringing them about, and the anxiety involved in giving up familiar behaviors and trying something new.

Therapists may also resist analysis of transference in the here and now. (1) Anxieties relating to the intensity of affect likely in a therapy that focuses on the here-and-now interaction may hinder the therapist. Discomfort with direct and immediate interchange may prompt its avoidance. It is often more comfortable to tone things down a bit and make a genetic interpretation rather than focus on the here-and-now interaction. (2) Analysis of transference in the here and now necessitates an active, give-and-take dialogue. The therapist traditionally trained in the use of "free association" and "evenly suspended attention" may feel uncomfortable with this in that such activity may be conceptualized as endangering neutrality and complicating transference development. (3) In striving to ascertain the extent to which a patient's reaction is based on transference or a realistic reaction to therapy, therapists all too often include all patient reactions to the therapist as transference. This may infantilize and infuriate. (4) The therapist may impede transference analysis by assuming a posture of certainty regarding the correctness of his interpretations. This interferes with the patient's ability to effectively collaborate. Ideas regarding relationship dynamics are best seen as hypotheses. (5) Therapists may move too quickly to analyze the nature of the patient's feelings for the therapist. Interventions need not prematurely force the patient to own his projections and displacements. Such defenses serve important intrapsychic functions.

This paper reflects the growing interest in a more interactional and interpersonal approach to transference analysis. Its illumination of resistances to such analysis is a unique and timely addition to an underdeveloped portion of the psychodynamic literature.

The term *transference*, as applied to the psychotherapeutic process, refers to the way in which the patient's view of and relations with childhood objects are expressed in current feelings, attitudes, and behaviors in regard to the therapist (Sandler et al. 1980). The analysis of transference is generally acknowledged as the central feature of psychodynamically oriented technique (Gill 1982). Such an analysis includes an interpretive focus on three situations: (1) the therapeutic situation involving clarification of the immediate here-and-now patient–therapist relationship, (2) the environmental interactions in present life, and (3) the childhood situation involving the carryover of the childhood past to the patient–therapist interaction. The classic transference interpretation reconstructs the past and explains how it affects the present patient–therapist interaction (Wisdom 1963).

Early trends in psychodynamic intervention emphasized understanding and reconstructing the genetic development of psychic conflict; technical interventions were geared to ensure the maximal development of the transference neurosis (Greenson 1967), which was seen as the most important vehicle of success in classical analytic technique (Freud 1912a/1958). An artifact of the analytic situation as engineered by Freud, the transference neurosis was facilitated by the use of the couch; daily sessions; therapist anonymity, nonintrusiveness, and passivity; and the rules of abstinence and free association (Fenichel 1941). In this approach the therapist was viewed as a neutral, opaque, relatively passive figure upon whom the patient's unresolved libidinal and aggressive conflicts were projected, thus allowing for their reconstruction and working through (Freud 1912a/1958). Although often effective in deepening the patient's self-understanding and sense of identity, the development of a regressive transference relationship emphasizing genetic recovery has been criticized as significantly lengthening treatment and resulting in less than optimal behavioral change (Alexander and French 1946, Malan 1963, 1976).

Of late there has been increased interest in a more active use of the transference relationship as a vehicle for modification of maladaptive coping strategies displaced onto the therapy situation (Bauer and Kobos 1987, Strupp and Binder 1984). This approach to the use of transference has been termed the "analysis of the transference in the here and now" (Gill 1982) and highlights the use of the current here-and-now relationship to clarify, examine, and modify interpersonal conflict rather than as a springboard for discussing the genetic determinants of conflict. An important impetus for development in the here-and-now use of transference comes from the burgeoning field of short-term psychotherapy. There has been a steady increase in interest and demand for effective modes of short-term treatment. Strupp and Binder (1984) contend that a focus on the here-and-now interaction is a critical component of technique in brief, dynamic psychotherapy. Bauer and Kobos (1984), in a review of major contributors to the development of short-term dynamic psychotherapy (i.e., Davanloo, Sifneos, Malan), found that the crucial change agent common to their techniques was an intensive emphasis on interpretation and working through of the transference relationship.

Work with transference in the here and now includes (1) sensitizing patients to the importance of examining their reactions to the therapist; (2) identifying the constricted, self-defeating components of these patterns; and (3) developing an increasingly flexible and mature interaction with the therapist. The focus is on transference reactions, or patterns of behavior that are transference based, rather than a systematic development and interpretation of a highly organized set of fantasies and attitudes displaced onto the therapist (i.e., the transference neurosis). Although existing on a continuum with the regressive transference neurosis, transference reactions are less organized, intense, and pervasive (Bauer and Kobos 1987). The here-and-now approach thus deemphasizes gaining access to repressed infantile conflict through intentional facilitation of a transference neurosis. Instead, major emphasis is placed on the examination and working through of characteristic patterns of relatedness (Strupp and Binder 1984) that are self-defeating and maladaptive.

The notion of a more vigorous here-and-now approach to transference is not new. As early as 1925, Rank and Ferenczi, in their classic volume on analytic technique, placed great importance on the identification and modification of maladaptive transference patterns in the therapy relationship. The work of such individuals as Reich (1933), Sullivan (1953), and more recently Davanloo (1978, 1980) has offered further support for this approach. Despite the theoretical attention given to understanding and resolving transference in the here and now, Gill (1982) contends that it is often underemphasized in practice.

Differences between theory and practice stem from resistances within both the patient and therapist. Resistance here refers to behavior in therapy that interferes with the processes of uncovering, affective expression, and working through of patient conflicts. While it is impossible to discuss all possible defensive mechanisms in a therapeutic relationship, the current work seeks to highlight key resistances to transference analysis. These resistances may be broken down (albeit somewhat artificially) into those stemming from the patient (patient-centered) and those of the therapist (therapist-centered).

PATIENT-CENTERED RESISTANCES

Patient resistance to here-and-now transference analysis is a pivotal issue in psychodynamic psychotherapy. Difficulties that may interfere with a patient's ability productively to examine the patient–therapist interaction include the patient's perception that the therapist is ignoring the patient's "real-world" problems, patient difficulties in identifying and accepting transference reactions, and the fears that arise when resolution of transference difficulties become associated with increasing autonomy and personal responsibility.

Ignoring Real-Life Concerns

An underlying premise of dynamic psychotherapy is that patients interact in a way that is generally consistent with their characteristic modes of functioning. A problem occurs, however, when the patient resists viewing a focus on the therapeutic interaction as an integral part of the treatment. Patients may feel that the therapist's attempt to examine the contemporary relationship is done at the expense of the "presenting problems" or other reality concerns. Gill (1982) contends that after initial discomfort with such a therapeutic stance, patients find it a great relief and an encouraging support to their autonomy that the therapist does not tell them how to live. In all cases, the most effective stance is one that stimulates the patient's curiosity regarding current functioning and encourages further exploration.

Identifying Transference

The dynamically oriented therapist seeks to develop latent transferential materials into manifest material for investigation. This is often a difficult task. In association with the anxiety accompanying self-exploration, patients may deny having reactions to the therapist and/or may actively discount their meaningfulness. The therapist can assist the patient in becoming more aware of transference by searching out allusions to transference in communications manifestly unrelated to the therapy relationship. Patients, for instance, may express the feeling that the therapist is critical and/or punitive by discussing a punitive parent, peer, or authority figure. Alternatively, the patient may become demeaning and self-critical by means of the defense of identification. The following example illustrates a patient's defensive style and a possible method of intervention.

Case Illustration

A middle-aged elementary school teacher (BT), sought therapy to work on self-assertion. In the eighth session, BT expressed intense anger with his supervising principal, stating that he was insensitive to students and teachers. BT further reported that the principal was quite rigid and overly structured in his work. The therapist was puzzled by the outburst as BT had thus far been rather controlled in his presentation as well as reporting satisfaction with his work environment and the supervisory relationship. The therapist was also aware that BT seemed more tense and distant in regard to the therapist during the past two sessions. As BT continued, the therapist noted parallels between BT's description of his supervisor and past comments about the therapist. In the fourth interview, for example, BT had commented on the orderliness of the therapist's office. To expand the patient's awareness of possible therapy-related implications of his anger, the therapist offered observations of possible parallels between himself and the principal. BT was initially resistant to such inquiry, however. After ventilation of his feelings seemed unsatisfying, BT acknowledged that his feelings extended beyond the person of the principal. Furthermore, the therapist's continued confrontation of the parallels helped BT to become aware of uncomfortable feelings toward the therapist. As work progressed, BT revealed that the discomfort had begun two sessions earlier when the therapist made what BT felt was an insensitive remark about BT's relationship with his wife.

The example of BT highlights the importance of the therapist noting concrete observations that are suggestive of here-and-now difficulties. The patient's confusing, self-defeating, and interpersonally distancing styles of relating are best focused on as they are concretely manifest in the relationship. When observations are made and the patient's means of relating is confronted, the patient experiences difficulties with increasing intensity, and motivation for the patient to modify his or her style is strengthened. The process of identification and illumination of specific behavior patterns fosters therapeutic gain and patient autonomy. While initial work with a transference theme may require substantial confrontation, the ability of a patient to address such themes increases each time the theme is examined. Patients can then work to relate in a more mature and productive manner. The therapist thus interacts with the patient as to encourage the patient's awareness and experience of his or her conflicted ways of relating as well as their consequences.

The work described with BT also points out the need for careful timing of the intervention. The therapist allowed BT to experience and express negative feelings to the extent that BT was able to recognize the broader implications of his feelings. The therapist's patience helped to create an environment that allowed the experience to intensify and helped BT feel that anxiety-provoking feelings could be risked. This *implicit* message of safety from the therapist is important in enhancing the therapeutic alliance and helping the patient risk examination of the here-and-now relationship.

Refusal to Consider the Possibility of Transference

Patients often resist exploration and working through of transference by staunchly maintaining the belief that their reactions to the therapist are based solely on the reality of the person of the therapist and that any interpersonal dilemmas are not related to intrapsychic conflict or past development. A patient, for example, may insist that all feelings toward the therapist, both positive and negative, are fully justified or explained by the conventionally viewed therapeutic situation. An inability to express oneself in treatment, as associated with a generally withholding and mistrustful character style, may be rationalized by attributing it to threatening features of the therapist or features of the therapeutic environment. The conclusion patients often want to believe is that there simply is no blind repeating of past patterns of relationship to be understood (Schafer 1983). Resistance of this type may be addressed by examination of historical parallels. Use of genetic material is most productively used to resolve impasses in the here-and-now relationship.

Fear of Autonomy

The refusal to examine transference reactions and to consider alternate ways of behaving with the therapist expresses a resistance to accepting responsibility for how one chooses to think and feel (Singer 1970). It is an escape from facing personal conflicts, the roles one has in bringing them about, and the anxiety associated with giving up secure, albeit neurotic and self-defeating mechanisms. The patient's avoidance of responsibility is often a fundamental concern in treatment. In some cases, it is a central feature.

Case Illustration

A patient (NB) presented with depression and pervasive feelings of isolation. Early in treatment NB revealed that one of her primary motivations for seeking therapy was to learn to cope with people whom she found to be cold, distant, and uncaring. As therapy progressed, the therapist became increasingly aware of how NB's frequent sarcasm and irritability made it difficult to feel very close to or involved with her. An educated, fastidious, and mannerly person, NB freely pointed out minor defects in the therapist's dress and manner of speaking. She regularly dismissed the therapist's comments and often referred to the unlikelihood that the therapist could actually be of help to her. NB was initially reluctant to engage in exploration of apparent tension in their relationship. However, this reluctance dissolved as NB began to have the same complaints about the therapist as she did of others (i.e., that they were distant and uncaring). Through careful examination and discussion of the means by which NB and the therapist related to each other, NB was able to see how her style contributed to her feeling isolated and distant. As NB was able to perceive that her approach to people in general was similar to her pattern with her therapist, it became increasingly difficult for her to see others as the sole cause of her painful relationships. Through such work, NB was encouraged to assume responsibility for her role in creating a life situation. This required her to relinquish externalizing, projective defenses, as well as whatever security (although maladaptive) they furnished.

THERAPIST-CENTERED RESISTANCE

In addition to patient-centered resistances, resistances within the therapist also contribute to an underemphasis of transference analysis in the here and now. Therapist-centered resistance may manifest in a variety of fashions including an avoidance of here-and-now affect, overemphasis on genetic investigation, limited therapist activity, difficulties in differentiating transference from nontransference behavior, presentation of a posture of certainty, and premature interpretation of patient projections. The sources of these resistances are complex, and may originate in the countertransference of the therapist, deficiencies in the training and supervision experiences of the therapist, or a complex interaction of these two important influences. This article does not propose to identify particular sources for the technical blocks discussed, but highlights the nature of some of the blocks that are possible in attempting to implement dynamically oriented psychotherapy. For the purpose of this discussion, countertransference refers to the therapist's emotional reactions to the patient developed during the treatment process. Such reactions stem from unresolved conflicts of the therapist, and/or the impact on the therapist of the patient–therapist interaction, especially the patient's conflicted interpersonal strategies (Bauer and Kobos 1987).

Avoidance of Here-and-Now Affect

It has been contended that the therapist's "faintheartedness" in discussing transference manifestations is responsible for more stagnation in dynamic therapy than for any other attitude (Glover 1955). The experience of examining transference in the here and now involves the patient and therapist in an affect-laden and potentially disturbing interaction. Fears associated with a direct, immediate interchange are often strong enough to encourage its avoidance.

A patient's perceptions of the therapist may be insightful and threatening. The increase in affect involved in here-and-now processing may stimulate the therapist's own conflictual areas and become problematic if the therapist has not successfully learned to manage his or her own conflicts. This is especially true when working with patients presenting seriously disturbed inter-personal relationships. Interacting with such individuals places an intense pressure on the adaptive defenses of the therapist that may result in ego regression and the acting out of conflicts by the therapist that had previously been mastered and modified (Kernberg 1975). The therapist's constructive means of dealing with such conflicts may be sorely tested as the therapist attempts to discuss and work through an especially anxiety-provoking impasse with the patient. In such cases, a therapist may unwittingly attempt to escape the intense pressure placed on adaptive defenses by shifting attention from the heat of the immediate situation to an exploration of past relationships. It is often more comfortable for the therapist to make a genetic connection than to focus on the here-and-now manifestations of transference. Epstein (1979) noted that although this strategy may succeed in quieting things down for the moment, it generally retards the working through of transference material.

Some therapists are reluctant to examine the patient–therapist interaction due to fear that a potentially difficult, anxiety-provoking work may interfere with the development of the therapeutic alliance. It is likely that the opposite is a better

reflection of reality. Inability of the therapist to confront troublesome aspects of the therapeutic interaction most often results
in the development of therapeutic impasse. Kernberg (1975)
stated that unless manifestations of the hostile, mistrustful components of transference are confronted early in treatment, there is
little development of a therapeutic alliance. Without a focus on
what impedes the patient–therapist collaboration, treatment is
at the mercy of the maladaptive and self-defeating ways in which
the patient reacts. Even though patients may "resist," they look to
the therapist for expert guidance and an honest experience in
order to enable work with their difficulties.

Overemphasis on Genetic Investigation

Although analysis of transference in the here and now focuses on
using the patient–therapist relationship to help the patient learn
about and resolve conflictual patterns of interaction, this should
not be misconstrued as negating the importance of understanding
the patient's developmental history. Attention to how conflictual
patterns have developed offers the patient a chance to understand and to connect across time the events of one's life. This
strengthens the patient's identity. It also creates confidence that
the patient's way of reacting may be understood and that one is
not involved in confused meandering through unrelated situations. Exploration of genetic material may also facilitate the
understanding and progressive modification of the present relationship. Rycroft (1966) notes that the therapist makes excursions
into historical research in order to understand something that is
interfering with present communication with the patient in the
same way that a translator might turn to history to elucidate an
obscure text. Though understanding of the past may be used to
decrease its harmful effects on the present, the therapist must
keep in mind that change rests on the reliving and modification of
meaningful patterns within the therapeutic interaction and not on
the elucidation of past events (Strupp 1973).

Constricted Therapist Activity

Here-and-now analysis of transference is facilitated by the creation of an active give-and-take dialogue that attempts to identify, examine, and modify neurotic patterns currently being enacted with the therapist. The traditional, dynamic therapist primarily trained in the use of quiet listening (i.e., evenly suspended attention; Freud 1912b/1958) and interpretation of free associations may feel uncomfortable with a more active engagement since activity has often been seen as endangering therapist neutrality and complicating transference development. Fenichel (1941) expressed concern that too much activity on the therapist's part would inhibit trust in the therapist and the patient's willingness to engage in a regression in service of the ego. He asserted that the therapist should strive to create an atmosphere of tolerance that expressed the implicit message: "You will not be punished here, so give your thoughts free rein." Through more active engagement, Fenichel saw the therapist as creating the possibility of becoming, in the unconscious of the patient, "a punisher, a repeater of childhood threats, or a magician waving away threats" (p. 86). The therapist's neutrality would be lost and the security of the therapeutic setting, so important in free-flowing communication, would be severely compromised. In addition to decreasing the security of the therapeutic environment, vigorous therapist interventions were thought to distort the natural development of transference, thus making these reactions more difficult to resolve. Such reasoning kept therapist interventions at a minimum with many opportunities to elicit change being overlooked.

The need to establish a safe, secure atmosphere in therapy and the importance of understanding the nature of transference reactions are essential therapeutic tasks. However, inhibiting one's therapeutic involvement (e.g., interpretation, confrontation, clarification) with the patient out of fear of transference distortion or a therapist's idiosyncratic interpretation of analytic theory does not make identification and use of transference reactions easier. Gill (1982) encouraged the therapist to keep in mind that the patient responds to what the therapist does *not* do, as well as to what he or she *does* do. The patient reacts to inactivity or unresponsiveness in the therapist, as well as to more active interventions. The silent, emotionally unresponsive therapist who gathers data and emits interpretations does no more supply the psychological milieu for the most undistorted delineation of the normal and abnormal features of a person's psychological makeup than does an oxygen-free atmosphere supply the physical milieu for the most accurate measurement of one's physiological responses (Kohut 1971). The stance of inhibiting one's responses may encourage the perception of the therapist as a cold, distant figure, regardless of the transference predisposition.

Difficulty in Differentiating Transference from Nontransference

It is important that patterns of interaction emerging from wishes and fears displaced onto the therapist be separated from the patient's realistic reactions to the treatment. That is, the therapist must work to discern the extent to which a patient reaction is based in transference. Thompson (1964) observed that therapists too often include all attitudes that a patient has toward the therapist as transference. Such a stance toward patient perceptions is often used defensively (Szasz 1963). It is clear that a patient may also have realistic reactions to treatment phenomena.

The difficulty in differentiating transference from nontransference reactions can be seen in a common example. There is a range of possible patient reactions (from apparent indifference to overt rage) when a therapist is late for a therapy appointment. Any particular reaction may be based in a range of psychic conditions. It is often difficult to separate the realistic irritation of a patient who feels that the appointment should begin at the agreed-upon (and paid for) time from the anger emanating from narcissistic injury. In discussing this dilemma, Lipton (1977) states, "The question of what part of the relationship is . . .

realistic and excluded from interpretation, and what part is unrealistic is usually obvious, but when it is not, there is nothing . . . to do except discuss the issue and settle it between them" (p. 268). Clarification of a patient's realistic reactions can deepen the therapeutic alliance and foster patient autonomy.

Presentation of a Posture of Certainty

As just discussed, the therapist and patient work to develop a consensually validated understanding of their relationship. The development of such understanding is a difficult task, since there is no context-free reality to use as a criterion for examining the relationship (Schafer 1983). Ideas regarding the dynamics of the relationship are best seen as hypotheses. Gill (1982) noted that exploring transference with the patient's frame of reference in mind decreases defensiveness and makes exploration more effective. A posture of "certainty" on the part of the therapist regarding what is transference and what is reality, or on what the patient is "really" saying interferes with the patient's ability to understand himself from a number of viewpoints. Such rigidity erodes the patient's ability to self-reflect in a healthy fashion. In discussing this issue, Lipton (1977) suggests that telling patients what they "really" mean is likely to be met with resistance and it is often more useful to suggest, for example, that what they are saying or doing may have implications for the therapy relationship.

Telling patients what they " really mean" can be an error of another type. To speak of "real" meaning disregards principles of multiple function and overdetermination (Waedler 1936). The fact that the therapist (or patient) has discerned further meaning, more disturbed meaning, or more carefully disguised meaning than that which first meets the eye or ear does not justify the claim that one has discovered the ultimate truth. A sounder claim would be that a point has been reached where reality must be formulated in a more subtle and complex manner than before (Schafer 1983).

Premature Interpretation of Projection

When discussing patient reactions to the therapy, it may not be as important to decide what is transference or nontransference, as it is for the patient to actively discuss perceptions of the therapist, and for the therapist to work with these perceptions in a nondefensive manner. Although reactions of the therapist are often strongly determined by the projection onto the therapist of internal self and/or object representations (Kernberg 1975), the therapist's interventions need not be designed to "force" the patient to own these projections. A therapist is ill advised to force a patient to relinquish prematurely defenses that serve an important function in psychic organization. Rather, it is often most helpful for the therapist to draw out the patient's feelings and to engage in a serious and nondefensive investigation of them. Epstein (1979) notes that such a stance conveys that the therapist (1) has a strong ego and is not harmed by the patient's projections, (2) has a desire to understand the patient's interpersonal and intrapsychic processes, and (3) is able to tolerate projections of unwanted (intolerable) aspects of the patient onto the self. This approach communicates trust in the therapeutic process and helps the patient gradually tolerate aspects of himself that were previously defended against by disavowal and projection. For example, a patient who has internalized a very critical and demanding parental object may become perfectionistic and demanding of himself with resulting depression, lack of satisfaction with life, and/or masochistic behavior. During therapy the patient may project this critical internal object onto the therapist and perceive the therapist as demanding and unforgiving. The patient may then relate to the therapist in a fashion used to relate to the original parent (e.g., appeasement, clinging, passive-aggression). The therapist's task is that of helping the patient discuss how the therapist is perceived and how this affects behavior. The therapist does not disown the patient's projections but rather attempts to study and understand. Such work helps detoxify unacceptable feelings and allows the patient to integrate rather than defend against them. The therapist is no longer viewed as critical, and patient and therapist are more able to collaborate on modifying the destructive components of the patient's internal objects (Epstein 1979).

SUMMARY

Ferenczi (1921/1950) suggested that most innovations in technique are not new and are already part of the practitioner's repertoire. While there has been considerable evolution in theoretical notions regarding the most efficacious use of transference in psychodynamically oriented treatment, the current work highlights difficulties in implementation of principles of technique.

Effective dynamic interventions may be hindered by fears and distortions in both the patient and the therapist. Patients may resist a shift from direct focus on real-world problems to the nature of the treatment relationship. Further, patients may be reluctant to face the possibility that experiences may be connected to feelings they have in relation to the therapy relationship. Similarly, it is difficult for patients to acknowledge that feelings they have in the therapy relationship may occur in the context of their characteristic tendencies of acting and reacting in important personal relationships. Finally, the implications of a patient's emergent autonomy may be a source of patient anxiety.

In addition to patient-oriented resistance to here-and-now transference analysis, this article discusses potential therapist difficulties with such work. Seen as often arising from therapists' own struggles, a number of therapist-centered blocks to here-and-now intervention are reviewed. Therapists may be limited by anxieties with the intensity of affect likely in a therapy that focuses on the here-and-now interaction. Confusion about work with historical material may lead to avoidance of the here-and-now material that may have a greater impact on therapeutic movement. Therapists may overly constrict activity as a way of maintaining security; they may also impede here-and-now work through difficulty separating a patient's transference-based reactions from nontransference reactions as well as interacting with patients from an overly certain stance. Finally, therapists may interfere with the therapy process by moving too quickly in analyzing the nature of the feelings the patient has for the therapist.

Analysis of transference in the here and now is an emotionally potent arena that can lead to resistance on the part of both the therapist and the patient. Both sources of resistance are important to address in attempting to build a therapeutic alliance and maximize treatment gains. Transference can be a powerful therapeutic tool in any therapy that involves a significant relationship between the therapist and patient. As a result, it is important to continue to be aware of blocks to effective intervention. In this way, training and supervision experiences can also be used in an optimal fashion.

REFERENCES

Alexander, F., and French, T. (1946). *Psychoanalytic Therapy: Principles and Applications*. New York: Ronald.

Bauer, G. P., and Kobos, J. P. (1984). Short-term psychodynamic psychotherapy: reflections on the past and current practice. *Psychotherapy* 21:153–170.

——— (1987). *Brief Therapy: Short-Term Psychodynamic Intervention*. New York: Jason Aronson.

Davanloo, H. (1978). *Basic Principles and Techniques in Short-Term Dynamic Psychotherapy*. New York: Spectrum.

——— (1980). *Short-Term Dynamic Psychotherapy*. New York: Jason Aronson.

Epstein, L. (1979). The therapeutic use of countertransference data with borderline patients. *Contemporary Psychoanalysis* 15:248–275.

Fenichel, O. (1941). *Problems of Psychoanalytic Technique*. New York: Psychoanalytic Quarterly.

Ferenczi, S. (1921 [1950]). Further development of an active therapy in psychoanalysis. In *Further Contributions to the Theory and Technique of Psychoanalysis*, ed. J. Suttie. London: Hogarth.

Freud, S. (1912a). The dynamics of transference. *Standard Edition*.

——— (1912b). Recommendations to physicians practicing psychoanalysis. *Standard Edition*.

Gill, M. (1982). *Analysis of Transference*. New York: International Universities Press.

Glover, E. (1955). *The Technique of Psychoanalysis*. New York: International Universities Press.

Greenson, R. (1967). *The Technique and Practice of Psychoanalysis*. New York: International Universities Press.

Kernberg, O. (1975). *Borderline Conditions and Pathological Narcissism*. New York: Jason Aronson.

Kohut, H. (1971). *The Analysis of the Self*. New York: International Universities Press.

Lipton, S. (1977). The advantages of Freud's technique as shown in his analysis of the Rat Man. *International Journal of Psycho-Analysis* 58:255–274.

Malan, D. (1963). *A Study of Brief Psychotherapy*. New York: Plenum.

_____ (1976). *Frontier of Brief Psychotherapy*. New York: Plenum.

Rank, O., and Ferenczi, S. (1925). *The Development of Psychoanalysis*. Trans. C. Newton. New York: Nervous and Mental Diseases Publishing Company.

Reich, W. (1933). *Character Analysis*. Trans. T. Wocfus. Rangeley, ME: Orgonics Institute Press.

Rycroft, C. (1966). *Psychoanalysis Observed*. London: Constable.

Sandler, J., Kennedy, H., and Tyson, R. (1980). *The Technique of Child Psychoanalysis: Discussions with Anna Freud*. Cambridge, MA: Harvard University Press.

Schafer, R. (1983). *The Analytic Attitude*. New York: Basic Books.

Singer, E. (1970). *Key Concepts in Psychotherapy*. Chicago: University of Chicago Press.

Strupp, H. (1973). *Psychotherapy: Clinical, Research, and Theoretical*. New York: Jason Aronson.

Strupp, H., and Binder, J. (1984). *Psychotherapy in a New Key*. New York: Basic Books.

Sullivan, H. S. (1953). *The Interpersonal Theory of Psychiatry*. New York: Norton.

Szasz, T. (1963). The concept of transference. *International Journal of Psycho-Analysis* 44:432–443.

Thompson, C. (1964). *Interpersonal Psychoanalysis*. New York: Basic Books.

Waelder, R. (1936). The principle of multiple function. *Psychoanalytic Quarterly* 5:45–62.

Wisdom, J. (1963). Psychoanalytic technology. In *Psychoanalytic Clinical Interpretation*, ed. L. Paul. New York: The Free Press.

Acknowledgments

The editor gratefully acknowledges permission to reprint the following:

"The Analysis of Transference," by Merton M. Gill, in *Journal of the American Psychoanalytic Association*, 1979, volume 27, pp. 263–288. Copyright © 1979 by International Universities Press. Reprinted by permission of International Universities Press and the author.

"Interpretation and Reality in Psychotherapy," by Sidney Tarachow, in *International Journal of Psycho-Analysis*, 1962, volume 43, pp. 377–387. Copyright © 1962 by *International Journal of Psycho-Analysis*; and "The Concept of Transference," by Thomas S. Szasz, volume 44, pp. 432–443. Copyright © 1963 by *International Journal of Psycho-Analysis*. Reprinted by permission of *International Journal of Psycho-Analysis* and the authors.

"Learning Theory and Psychoanalysis," by Eugene Wolf, in *British Journal of Medical Psychology*, 1966, volume 39, pp. 1–10. Copyright © 1966 by The British Psychological Society. Reprinted by permission.

"The Dynamics of Transference," by Sigmund Freud, from *The Collected Papers*, volume 2. Authorized translation under the supervision of Joan Riviere. Published by Basic Books, Inc. by arrangement with the Hogarth Press, Ltd. and The Institute of Psycho-Analysis, London. Reprinted by permission of Basic Books, a division of HarperCollins Publishers Inc., Sigmund Freud Copyrights, The Institute of Psycho-Analysis, and the Hogarth Press.

"Transference and Information Processing," by Drew Westen, in *Clinical Psychology Review*, 1989, volume 8, pp. 161–179. Copyright © 1989 by Pergamon Press Ltd., Oxford, England. Reprinted by permission.

Excerpts from "The Patient as Interpreter of the Analyst's Experience," by Irwin Z. Hoffman, in *Contemporary Psychoanalysis*, 1983, volume 19, pp. 389–422. Copyright © 1983 by *Contemporary Psychoanalysis*; and "Patterns of Influence in the Analytic Relationship" (originally entitled "From Neutrality to Personal Revelation: Patterns of Influence in the Analytic Relationship") by Paul Wachtel, volume 22, pp. 60–70. Copyright © 1986 by *Contemporary Psychoanalysis*. Reprinted by permission of *Contemporary Psychoanalysis*.

"Patient and Therapist Resistance to Use of the Transference in the Here and Now" (originally entitled "Use of Transference in the Here and Now: Patient and Therapist Resistance") by Gregory P. Bauer and John A. Mills, in *Psychotherapy*, 1989, volume 26, pp. 112–119. Copyright © 1989 by *Psychotherapy*. Reprinted by permission.

Index

Blank screen concept. *See also*
Patient interpretation
paradigms and critiques,
88–90
resilience of, 83–86
standard qualifications of,
86–88
Bleuler, E., 15
Blum, H. P., 46
Bollas, C., 102n7, 103
Borderline personality disorder
interpersonal expectancies and,
33
transference and, 44
Bower, G. H., 34, 42
Bowlby, J., 29
Brenner, C., 36
Breuer, J., 182–186, 187, 188, 189,
190, 192

Cantor, N., 27, 28
Cathexis, transference and, 8,
32
Certainty, posture of,
therapist-centered
resistance, 209
Clark, D. M., 42
Cognition
information processing and,
19–51. *See also* Information
processing
reality and, 90
sexuality and, 43
Cognitive-behavioral perspective,
transference and, 19
Coleman, J. V., 144
Collins, A. M., 37
Conflict behavior,
psychodynamic model of
learning, 56

Consciousness
introversion and, 10–11
resistance and, 10–12
Countertransference
enactment and confession of,
101–103
inevitability of, 95–96
neutrality and, 73
psychodynamic model of
learning, 58
social paradigm and, 97–99
therapist-centered resistance,
204
Criminality, mental illness and,
60
Crocker, J., 27

Data types, analytic situation
and, 176–178
Davanloo, H., 195, 198, 199
Defenses
affect-regulation mechanisms,
reworking of, information
processing, 45–46
of analyst, transference concept
and, 175–192
ego structure and, 142
information processing
perspective, 38–40
psychotherapy and, 160
transference as, 178–182
Denial, transference and,
188–190
Derry, P. A., 42
Deutsch, H., 147
Dewald, P. A., 86n3
Displacement, interpretation and
reality, 157–159
Dreams, unconscious and, 17